Helen Bishop

'A Pearl of the Kingdom'

Her Spiritual Journey

Nosrat'ullah Rassekh

Helen Bishop

Publication Copyright © National Spiritual Assembly of the Bahá'ís of Australia Inc. All Rights Reserved

Text Copyright © Nosrat'ullah Rassekh

Bahá'í Publications Australia
ISBN 978-1-923266-18-6 (softcover)
ISBN 978-1-923266-19-3 (hardcover)
ISBN 978-1-923266-20-9 (ePub)
First edition, April 2025

Distributed by
Bahá'í Distribution Services
173 Mona Vale Rd, Ingleside, NSW, 2101
bds@bahai.org.au
www.bahaibooks.com.au

Title text typeset in Didot LT Pro
Body text typeset in 12/17pt Minion 3
Other text typeset in Avenir Next

Special thanks to Don Rassekh and Hillary Chapman for their assistance with publishing

Bahá'í
Publications
Australia

Contents

Context	ix
Prelude	xiii
Introduction	1

Chapter 1 : The Highest Truth — 11

The Valley of Search	13
The Latimers	17
A Tutor for Mary Maxwell	23
Marriage, College, and Pilgrimage	28

Chapter 2 : The International Bahá'í Bureau — 33

The Cradle of the League of Nations	35
In the Presence of the Guardian	40
The World Congress of Faiths	50
The Marriage of Shoghi Effendi	61
In Praise of Words	64
Farewell to Europe	67

Photos	71
Chapter 3 : Return to America	**91**
The Seven Year Plan	93
North to Alaska	102
Life on the Road	107
The British Baháʼí Community and the War	109
The Seven Year Plan : Latin America	118
The Seven Year Plan : Home Front	120
The Passing of Mrs May Maxwell	124
Chapter 4 : America At War	**129**
Purified in the Crucible of a Common War	131
A Visit with Shoghi Effendi's Oxford Tutor	137
An Encounter with Dr Jordan	142
1944 : The Centennial Celebration	148
Chapter 5 : Finding Home	**159**
Concerns for Helen's Health	161
The Beloved Returns	162
1946: The Second Seven Year Plan	165
His Japanese Witnesses	172
1948 : For the Faith—Two Great Triumphs	176

A Home at Last !	178
'Introduction' to the Book of Certitude	182
Helen's Studies of Judaism	184
Chapter 6 : Latter Years	**187**
The Inauguration of the Ten-Year World Crusade	189
The Ten-Year Plan	195
The Passing of the Guardian	199
Charles' Passing	202
Resignation from the Portland Assembly	205
Endnotes	209

Dedicated to my dear wife Mona
and my children, Billy, Suzie,
Paree and Michael

Nosrat'ullah Rassekh

Context

Professor Nosrat'ullah Rassekh was a devoted Bahá'í and a beloved professor of history at Lewis and Clark College in Oregon. Born in Tehran, Iran, he immigrated to the United States in 1944 as part of a group of young Iranian scholars seeking higher education. He earned his PhD in American intellectual history from Stanford University and went on to teach at Lewis and Clark for thirty-one years. During his tenure, he served as Head of the History Department and led student study trips to Mexico, Iran, and Egypt. Even after retiring, he remained dedicated to education, teaching summer and graduate courses. Under his leadership, the department became an early pioneer in introducing courses on African American history and women's history.

To his many friends, Professor Rassekh—affectionately known as 'Nas'—was more than an educator; he was a pillar of the Bahá'í community. For years, he served on the Spiritual Assembly of Portland, Oregon, where he worked alongside Helen Bishop, one of the most dynamic Bahá'í speakers and teachers of her time. Helen travelled extensively, spreading the teachings of the Faith, lecturing around the world, and playing a crucial role in organizing the Bahá'í office in Geneva. Nas held her in great esteem, and his deep respect for her life's work inspired him to document her remarkable journey. The book that follows is the result of his meticulous research and a heartfelt tribute to a dear friend whose service to the Cause left a lasting impact.

At the time of Professor Rassekh's passing in 2014, the book was largely complete but required further editing and source verification. Thanks to the dedication of his nephew, Donoush Rassekh, the manuscript has been carefully prepared for publication. Many individuals contributed to bringing this project to fruition, including Rosanne Adams (Eliot, Maine), Payam Afsharian (Los Angeles), Merat Bagha and Maura Fox (Portland), all of whom assisted in tracking down archival sources. Sheila Banani generously provided personal documents, while Barbara Klingsporn (San Francisco) and Guy Olson contributed significantly to editing. Tulsi Ramchandani played a crucial role in organizing and compiling materials for Professor Rassekh, and Edward Sevcik from the US National Bahá'í Archives provided valuable archival support.

In certain footnotes, the phrase 'archive unknown' appears. This notation indicates that the original source material could not be located. However, the quoted content has been retained, as it is certain that Professor Rassekh had access to these sources, even if the original documents have since been misplaced. It is possible that a folder of materials has gone missing over time.

We are honoured to present this completed work, which chronicles the life of Helen Bishop, one of the most distinguished Bahá'ís of her time. Through her story, readers will gain insight into the lives and struggles of her contemporaries—May Maxwell and her daughter, Mary Maxwell (later Amatu'l-Bahá Rúhíyyih Khánum, wife of Shoghi Effendi), Honor Kempton (founder of the Bahá'í community of Alaska), the Latimers (who introduced Helen to the Faith), and Marion Holley (an American Baha'i who served on the National Spiritual Assembly of the United Kingdom and homefront pioneered to various cities there), among many others. These individuals laboured tirelessly to spread the teachings of Bahá'u'lláh, strengthening Bahá'í communities across the world.

It is with deep appreciation for Professor Rassekh's work and vision that we share this book with you.

Hillary Ioas Chapman

Washington, DC, 2022

Prelude

This moving narrative, written by my dear uncle, Nasrollah Rassekh, tells the story of Helen Bishop, a distinguished early Bahá'í teacher. Helen's dedication and service to the Faith led to her appointment as Director of the International Bahá'í Bureau in Geneva, a role she accepted with a great sense of responsibility. In recognition of her abilities, the Guardian wrote to her:

> *You are the right person who is needed now that the International Bahá'í Bureau is acquiring an important international status in the administration.*

Helen's influence on the Bahá'í community was profound. May Maxwell, in a heartfelt letter, described Helen's spiritual radiance:

> *You are a pearl of the kingdom. As the Master said, 'a pearl of great price,' and you will affect profoundly the main springs and sources of the spiritual life and inspiration of the Cause…*

Similarly, Louis Gregory expressed his admiration in a letter to Helen, recognizing her rare gifts:

It has already been my good fortune to see one so illumined at so tender an age ... God has been infinitely kind to imbue you with His Knowledge, and you have shown gratitude by your wish to inspire and help others in the pathway of the all-beauteous Light.

My uncle, Nas—as he was lovingly known by his students—was among a remarkable group of nine Iranian Bahá'ís who arrived on the West Coast of the United States during World War II. This distinguished group included Firuz Kazemzadeh, Amin Banani, Shidan Fatheazam, and others. Upon their arrival, they had the privilege of meeting early Bahá'í pioneers, including Helen Bishop. Through Nas's eyes, this book beautifully bridges the achievements of the early Bahá'í believers with the next generations who carried forward their legacy.

Having lived and studied in Oregon, I had the privilege of knowing Helen in the later years of her life. I was blessed to assist her with everyday tasks—shopping, doctors' appointments—and attend her inspiring firesides. I have never met a more charming, distinguished, and knowledgeable individual.

One of the most profoundly moving moments of my life came while I was serving as a pioneer in Mali. The US Embassy informed me of Helen's passing, and to my astonishment, I learned that she had left a sum in her will toward the education of my children, Neysan and Bahie. Words cannot express the depth of my emotion at this final act of generosity from someone who had already given so much.

Helen Bishop's story is one of passion, courage, and unwavering dedication—a powerful reminder of the lasting impact one person can have on the world. To quote the words of Shoghi Effendi, written in a letter to Helen:

> *You have set an example which your fellow believers will be inspired to emulate.*

It is my honour to share this book with you, in memory of Helen's extraordinary life and in gratitude to my dear uncle, Nas, for preserving her legacy.

Donoush Rassekh

Virginia, 2022

Introduction

On 19 September 1977, in a letter to Mrs Edna True, Helen Bishop wrote:

> *For sometime I have been reviewing my papers. Our Persian friends Firuz [Kazemzadeh] and Nas Rassekh and his brother have tried to persuade me to [write my memoirs]. Finally the very learned Mr. Shapour Rassekh inspired me by saying that I should write down all that I remember of the 'Heralds of the Covenant' [for posterity].*[1]

However, it was the hope of these 'Persian friends' that Helen herself would one day write her own life story, preserving it for future generations. Having embraced the Faith of Bahá'u'lláh early in her life, Helen devoted herself to its service, both at home and abroad. For nearly four years (1934–1937), under the specific direction of Shoghi Effendi, she oversaw the International Bahá'í Bureau in Geneva, Switzerland. While on this assignment, she travelled extensively across Europe, sharing with audiences both large and small, the teachings of God's latest Revelation.

At a time when the world was on the brink of catastrophe, Helen tirelessly conveyed Bahá'u'lláh's promise of world peace. As international anarchy and dictatorship gained momentum, she spoke passionately about a divinely ordained World Order. While oppressive regimes trampled on human rights, she boldly emphasised the noble station of humankind and the God-given rights of all people.

In Germany, under the watchful eye of the Gestapo, Helen continued her work with courage and steadfastness, representing the Bahá'í Faith with unwavering dedication—until she was denied a visa, and all Bahá'í institutions in the country were banned.

Helen returned to the United States in the autumn of 1937. The world was on the precipice of World War II, and the prophetic words of Bahá'u'lláh, written two generations earlier, were becoming evident:

> *Soon will the present-day order be rolled up, and a new one spread in its stead.*

Despite the darkness that enveloped the world, there were glimmers of hope—the birth of a new world order to replace the crumbling old one.

During the darkest hours of World War I (March–April 1916), 'Abdu'l-Bahá—the Centre of Bahá'u'lláh's Covenant—addressed eight Tablets to the Bahá'ís of North America, urging them to spread the Faith:

> *… the fame of the Cause of God may be diffused throughout the East and the West and the advent of the Kingdom of the Lord of Hosts be proclaimed in all the five continents of the globe.*[2]

At that time, the United States had not yet entered the Great War, but 'Abdu'l-Bahá called upon its small Bahá'í community to

> ... *increase a thousandfold* ... [3]

their efforts to bring the Healing Message of Bahá'u'lláh to suffering humanity, promising that:

> *Should you become confirmed therein, this world will become another world, the surface of the earth will become the delectable paradise, and eternal Institutions be founded.*[4]

At the time, the Bahá'í Faith was still relatively new in the United States and Canada, having only been introduced less than thirty years earlier. It was first publicly mentioned at the 1893 Columbian Exposition in Chicago by a Christian missionary who had lived in the Middle East. Yet, remarkably, by 1900, the Faith had spread to twenty-one states and one Canadian province.

While still small in numbers (with an estimated 1,500 believers at the time), the Bahá'í community included dedicated figures such as:

- Thornton Chase
- Arthur Pillsbury Dodge
- Howard McNutt
- James and Isabella Brittingham
- Sarah Farmer
- Helen Goodall
- WR Randall
- Phoebe Hearst (mother of publishing titan William Hearst)

Among these early followers of Bahá'u'lláh was also Robert Turner, Mrs Hearst's butler, who became the first Bahá'í of African-American descent.

Helen Bishop: A Shining Star

Helen Bishop belonged to this illustrious generation—a shining star among its ranks. She first heard about Bahá'u'lláh in San Francisco at the age of seventeen. But it was not until three years later, in Portland, that she officially embraced the Faith, committing her life to its service.

From that moment forward, Helen's love for the Faith was unwavering. May Maxwell, in a letter to her, observed:

> *That while on earth the beloved Master found few capable of understanding or feeling, and those He did find cherished it as His most sacred heritage and the living remnant of Himself.* [5]

In 1926, the National Bahá'í Convention for the election of the National Spiritual Assembly of North America was held in San Francisco. Once the convention ended, several prominent Bahá'í teachers, scholars, and administrators visited Portland, where Mrs Maxwell remained for three weeks. These included:

- Corinne True
- Roy Wilhelm
- Albert Vail
- May Maxwell

- Louis Gregory
- Elizabeth Greenleaf

Helen, still in the early years of her Bahá'í journey, had the privilege of meeting these remarkable souls—an experience that profoundly shaped her life. Yet what was equally remarkable was the lasting impression she left on those she encountered.

In 1926 from Eliot, Maine, Louis Gregory—a future Hand of the Cause of God—who had just met Helen, wrote to her:

> *Guide my dear child, the young and old, the wise and foolish, the guilty and just. Transform their lives by the Elixir of life. If you live for a thousand years in this world, you could not select a work that is fraught with more far-reaching and eternally happy results. It is a path of difficulty too, but for this reason all the more glorious as you remain firm and steadfast you can always count upon the Supreme Power of Universe to sustain your efforts. You have something to offer famished souls and if you continue will leave bright traces even in this dark world to say nothing of the world beyond which are bright and luminous.*[6]

Upon returning home to Maine, Louis Gregory, in a letter dated 7 June 1926, praised Helen, writing:

> *It has rarely been my good fortune to see one so illumined at so tender age ... God has been infinitely kind to imbue you with His knowledge and you have shown your gratitude by*

your wish to inspire and help others to the pathway of all beauteous Light.[7]

Likewise, May Maxwell, writing to Helen while travelling from Seattle to Montreal, expressed:

I am only one insignificant servant of the Holy Threshold, yet twice it has happened to me since I left Portland that your pure face and eyes have appeared vividly before me during prayer, calling me to a height for which I have yearned but been unable to attain. Are we not linked in an infinite chain drawing each other even higher toward the One who holds us in His grasp and this chain forged the souls of His servants will draw all humanity?[8]

This was the life Helen lived—one of service, dedication, and unwavering faith.

'No doubt I would be living within the closed circle of small duties had not my life been seized and swung into the flow of the Cause. My first existence was vanished into a second in His Faith, which overrides my temperament and disinclinations: it makes me to do what I am not big enough to achieve, it brings me an insistence that I—without literary pretensions—dare my pen on the theme which is the secret of all pertinent themes of our time, for as much as each universe of discourse has been conditioned today by world-destroying consequences and rebirth that attends the Arrival of the Lord of Hosts.'

Helen Bishop, *The Beloved Returns*[9]

Chapter 1

THE HIGHEST TRUTH

Chapter 1

The Valley of Search

Helen Pilkington was born in July 1904 in Mazatlán, Mexico. Her mother, María, was Mexican, and her great-grandfather had been a Spanish viceroy in Mexico. Her father, Guy Pilkington, was an American mining engineer who had travelled to Mexico for work. There, he fell in love with the beautiful María, married her, and settled in Mazatlán.

Helen was the third of the couple's six children who survived birth. In 1908, the family made the difficult decision to move to the United States when their eldest son contracted the bubonic plague. Portland, Oregon—Guy's native city—became their new home.

From a young age, Helen displayed exceptional intelligence and deep spirituality. At just five years old, her parents decided to enrol her in a convent school, but her father soon had second thoughts. Concerned that she might one day become a nun, he withdrew her. Yet, despite her short time there, the experience left an indelible mark on the sensitive child.

Nearly two decades later, in a letter to her college friend, Honor Kempton, Helen recalled an experience from those early years:

> *I was only five, at the convent, when I slipped into church early one morning. The body of a young priest was lying before the altar, prepared for the burial. Others came into sanctuary and a service was held. Nobody paid any attention to me, or I did not become aware of others. I understood the words that were spoken for the soul, and more that was not. I became enamored of the mystery of death, although not with the escape from life sense. In any case, as a child my walks always carried me to graveyards, where I felt neither sorrow nor joy, only the awareness of the quietness in all things and the freedom to be.*[10]

This curiosity about life after death became deeply embedded in Helen's psyche. As she later explained, it was not necessarily an indication of her spirituality. Faith, however, remained a defining element of her character. She later wrote to Marion Holley:

> *You know that I am trying to be objective about my make-up, as about the weather ... Certainly such a complete acceptance of there-is-a-God, I will-live-forever were my data of my consciousness by the time I was four ... I prayed with tears and felt God saw every one of them. Once I found a dime, struggled towards the sweets we did not have very often, and yet I went alone into the chapel at the convent and put it into the Virgin's box and asked her to make me better.*[11]

Yet, despite her devotion, Helen was a spirited child with a fierce temper. She recalled:

... withal this acceptance of the Word of God reaching down in to the everyday world, I was the meanest kid on the block. I told lies. I cheated at games ... the relation with others was weak. In [a] fit of rage I would dash myself to the floor screaming, even to my father of whom I was afraid. 'Nobody loves me. I won't live in this world. Awful world! I will throw myself before the street car. Then I will be with the little Lord Jesus ...' Mind was at the minimum. Poor student always. Day dreaming, wishful thinking getting into the way of everything, both the mathematical and historical sense.[12]

A Mind Shaped by Literature

From an early age, Helen was an avid reader, drawn to romantic novels. As a teenager, she admitted she relied too much 'upon the rhythm of life and felt little need for approaching its problems rationally.'[13]

At eleven years old, she read and fell in love with Anna Karenina. She later reflected on how the conflict between will and desire remained a dominant theme in her young life

and the mind did not arrive until late. In fact I became a Bahá'í without it.[14]

But once the Bahá'í Faith became part of her consciousness, everything changed. She began

to absorb the Teachings as [I]... had done the novels.[15]

Spiritual Awakening

> *I cannot remember the time when God was not the first reality to me*[16]

Helen wrote these words to Honor Kempton on 14 December 1939, recalling how she first heard about Bahá'u'lláh eighteen years earlier, at the age of seventeen.

It was 1921, and Helen was in San Francisco. On the very eve of 'Abdu'l-Bahá's ascension, she attended a public meeting at the Fairmont Hotel, where Orcella Gregory spoke about God's newest Revelation.

Helen heard the Message that night—but it did not immediately penetrate her soul.

Three years later, however, in Portland, a personal crisis forced Helen to re-evaluate her life's purpose. She had been engaged to be married, but her fiancé unexpectedly broke off the engagement. The heartbreak was devastating. In her moment of despair, she turned to God

> *... and asked for the highest Truth of my time with the promise that I would give my life for its service.*[17]

Seven days later, everything changed. Helen described the moment her world was transformed:

... my new world was created; for I heard the Teachings from the Latimers. That is they gave me the Books. The picture of the Master had convinced me: stirring a vague recollection of I know what not—even to this day. And tears and repentance ... In about two months, I put pieces together and went back to school, where I had a history of failure.[18]

The Latimers

The Latimers—James and Harriett (Rouhani)—were distinguished and longtime Bahá'ís from Oregon who regularly held firesides at their home. There could not have been a clearer channel to connect Helen Bishop to the Bahá'í Faith than this remarkable couple.

Their son, George Latimer, had the privilege of meeting 'Abdu'l-Bahá in 1912 during His travels in the United States. Determined to see the Master, George took a six-day train journey from Portland to Dublin, New Hampshire, where 'Abdu'l-Bahá was staying. He arrived at 3:00 pm on 29 July, and just an hour later, at 4:00 pm, he was introduced to the Master. 'Abdu'l-Bahá warmly greeted him, recalling that He had previously met George's parents in Chicago.

A Treasured Encounter with 'Abdu'l-Bahá

During his visit, George Latimer kept a diary, carefully recording his experiences with 'Abdu'l-Bahá. One entry, written at Mrs Parsons' house, recounts how 'Abdu'l-Bahá inquired about the Portland Bahá'ís: 'Are the souls progressing in Portland? … are they advancing or stationary?' Then He commented: 'stagnation is the beginning of retrogression.' On another occasion, when Mrs Hoag, Mrs Kline and George were with the Master, He told them that they could record what he said, however He asked that He sign the notes in as much as He had been misquoted before.[19]

One morning, 'Abdu'l-Bahá spoke to George Latimer on the porch of the inn, offering encouragement in his teaching work and urging him to remain steadfast:

> *The Bahai must first be informed of the Principles and Teachings of BAHA'O'LLAH, then go forth and spread the Message. It is like unto a soldier, who must arm himself with the buckler and armor, and then he enters the battlefield to fight against the foe. But if he goes to fight without arming himself, he will be defeated. The Bahais are the Army of God. Their defensive armors or weapons are: First, Faith; second, Assurance; third, Severance; fourth, Complete Attraction to the Kingdom of ABHA. If they are armed with these weapons, they will gain the victory in whatever field they may enter.*[20]

The encounter left such a profound impact on young George that he resolved to dedicate his life to the service of the Faith.

A Journey of Service

In early 1914, George travelled to Europe to teach the Faith, eager to share the message of the Great Redeemer of mankind. When World War I erupted in August 1914, he found himself in Germany. Remarkably, he wrote to his parents about the unexpected opportunities he had to share the Bahá'í Message with soldiers.

Together with another American, Mason Remey, and several Persian Bahá'ís, George departed for Palestine, arriving in Haifa on 4 October 1914. The two Americans remained there for two weeks.*

On 17 October, Shoghi Effendi was preparing to set sail for Beirut to continue his education. That evening, he dined with several friends, including George, before making his way down to the docks. Just before boarding an Italian steamer bound for Lebanon, Shoghi Effendi gifted George a small photograph of the Master, with an inscription in his own handwriting:

> *As a token of Bahá'í love and sincere greetings to my dear friend, George Latimer from Shoghi Rabbani.*

Two days later, on 19 October, George and Mason Remey went to bid farewell to 'Abdu'l-Bahá. The Master's final words to them were:

---

* It was during his visit in Haifa in 1914 that George first met Shoghi Effendi, the seventeen-year-old grandson of 'Abdu'l-Bahá. He was immediately impressed by the charm and the intellect of the future Guardian of his Faith, and a strong bond was established between the two. On several occasions, they walked from the Shrine of the Bab to the marketplace, and as they walked, they discussed many subjects (author's note).

Praise to God that you are heralds of the Kingdom of God ... The popularity of the worldly heralds may last for a year or two, but the fame of the souls who are the heralds of the Kingdom is eternal, for they are sounding the trumpet of celestial universal peace ... Now I desire to send you back to the United States. I supplicate and beseech at the Threshold of the kingdom of Abha that you may go forth into the world with a heavenly power, with radiant heart ... I anticipate receiving glad-news from you.

George carefully documented each day of his pilgrimage in his diary, recording 'Abdu'l-Bahá's words and guidance. However, on 10 October, when he fell ill with stomach troubles, he asked Mason Remey to take notes on his behalf. That evening, Mason handed him the pages, including this important passage. Remey notes:

After a few preliminary remarks, the Master read to us numerous quotations from the writings of Bahá'u'lláh concerning the protection of the Cause of God — holding aloof from those who are the violators of the Cause of God, including passages from Persian Hidden Words: 'Preserve this servant from the instigation of those who have turned away from thee.' 'Abdu'l-Bahá also quoted from the Tablet of Question where Bahá'u'lláh prays 'I ask Thee O Possessor of Names and the Creator of Heaven ... to reinforce me with the Standards of Thy Power and Might, protecting me from the weakness of Thy enemies who have violated Thy Will and Testament.'

If only the hearer could have heard the Message.

At the conclusion of their pilgrimage, 'Abdu'l-Bahá blessed the two young men, saying:

> *May you be confirmed and assisted and may you raise such a melody and sing such a song as to stir and move the hearts of the American people.*

Upon his return to the United States, George devoted his life to teaching the Faith. Years later, it was in his home that Helen Bishop first heard 'the melody" of the Bahá'í Message—the answer to the prayer she had made in her darkest hour, seeking 'the highest Truth.'

Meeting the Pioneers of the Faith

Shortly after Helen's conversion, she had the opportunity to meet and befriend some of the most prominent Bahá'ís of her time.

In 1926, the National Bahá'í Convention was held in San Francisco for the election of the National Spiritual Assembly of the Bahá'ís of North America. After the convention, a number of attendees stopped in Portland before returning home, including:

- Corinne True
- Horace Holley
- Roy Wilhelm
- Albert Vail
- Louis Gregory
- May Maxwell
- Elizabeth Greenleaf

Mrs Maxwell remained in Portland for three weeks, and Helen had the privilege of meeting and learning from these remarkable souls. But just as Helen was deeply inspired by them, these veteran Bahá'ís were equally moved by the young woman's charm, intellect, and spirit.

After her visit, Mrs Maxwell wrote from Seattle, sending Helen a letter filled with warmth and encouragement:

> … you are a pearl of the Kingdom. As the Master said 'a pearl of great price,' and you will affect profoundly the main springs and sources of the spiritual life and inspiration of the Cause … Do write to me my precious one … and share with me any great tidings that you have, for the praise of such a heart as yours refreshes and revives the traveler and wayfarer in the path of God … I am only one insignificant servant of the Holy Threshold, yet twice it has happened to me since I left Portland that your pure face and eyes have appeared vividly before me during prayer, calling me to a height for which I have yearned but been unable to attain. Are we not linked in an infinite chain drawing each other toward the One who holds us in His grasp and this chain forged in the souls of His servants will draw all humanity?[21]

In the same letter, Mrs Maxwell informs Helen that she sent her a copy of the *Unveiling of the Divine Plan* 'so that you may receive directly from that Mighty Source of humanity for your inspiration to carry on the work in the field.'[22]

Ten days later, writing from Vancouver, BC, Mrs Maxwell reaffirmed Helen's deep love for the Faith:

> ... that while on earth the beloved Master found few capable of understanding or feeling, and those He did find cherished it as His most sacred heritage and the living remnant of Himself.[23]

Around the same time, Louis Gregory also wrote to Helen, expressing his admiration:

> It has rarely been my good fortune to see one so illumined at so tender age ... God has been infinitely kind to imbue you with His knowledge and you have shown gratitude by your wish to inspire and help others to the pathway of all beauteous Light.[24]

A Tutor for Mary Maxwell

From Portsmouth, New Hampshire, some two months later, Mrs Maxwell wrote candidly to Helen, sharing her deep concerns about the spiritual state of the American Bahá'í community:

> ... [the Cause in America] is a body without a soul, an organization but not a living, breathing organism.[25]

She then added:

> ... there is a profound significance in our knowing you in Portland, for various reasons I cling to terms of moderation in this connection, but words are not needed between you and me. We [the National Spiritual Assembly of North America] have reached two conclusions, that H. [Horace Holley] must go to Haifa this Fall as a representative of the N.S.A. and having established that vital connection with the Divine Beloved return to the 'Heart of the Cause in America,' as Shoghi Effendi calls the N.S.A. The other point, dearest, is this. Do you think you could tutor Mary, my sixteen-year-old daughter this winter?[26]

It seems that Mrs Maxwell was suddenly inspired by the idea. In her letter, she explained that a year earlier (1925), the Maxwell family had visited Shoghi Effendi in Haifa. One day during their visit, while the parents were conversing with the beloved Guardian, he had suggested that their young daughter Mary should dedicate three to four hours a day to her studies, covering all subjects of general and broad education in its modern form. According to a letter from Mary Maxwell to her mother, Shoghi Effendi had advised:

> ... [He] wanted me to get a good general education first and then ... to take some lectures in some good college on either Economics or sociology or literature.[27]

This visit to Haifa had been a turning point for young Mary, bringing a profound shift in her consciousness. When the Maxwells returned to Canada, they consulted on finding a tutor to support their daughter's education.

At first, they had chosen an elderly woman who was a great educator and had already recommended several excellent books while meeting with Mary a few times. However, Mary found the woman's perspective too narrow, leading her parents to reconsider their choice.[28]

After meeting Helen in Portland, Mrs Maxwell became convinced that Helen would be an ideal tutor. She wrote:

Besides, Mary already loves you, and when [I] suggested the plan to her, she beamed with joy ... Should you decide on the wisdom of this plan, or, at least on your willingness to give it a trial, we can discuss arrangements and financial detail in my reply to you.[29]

However, upon further reflection, the parents realised a potential challenge: the closeness in age and friendship between pupil and tutor. They feared this might compromise the discipline necessary for an effective teacher-student relationship. Mrs Maxwell, thinking about Mary's experience in Haifa, wrote:

... such true love for the Guardian, such a sincere and intense desire to study and become educated in the way that he wishes that, knowing her temper as I do, I for one believe it necessary to leave her quite free on the choice of her teachers that is, of course, if the right person can be found ... Mary it seems has been thinking along the line of a man tutor. She

feels that she could do her best work with a man, that he would put an unconscious check on certain temperamental tendencies which she knows well in the past have interfered with her sincere study.[30]

Thus, the idea of Helen becoming Mary's tutor was ultimately set aside. Instead, the Maxwells approached a professor from McGill University, and by autumn 1926, Mary Maxwell officially enrolled at McGill University in Montreal.

A New Bahá'í Centre and an Unforgettable Friendship

In November 1926, Mrs Maxwell had 'four heavenly days' with Juliet Thompson, the accomplished artist and renowned Bahá'í, before Juliet departed for Washington, DC, to paint a portrait of First Lady Grace Coolidge, wife of President Calvin Coolidge, in the White House.

Juliet was eager for Mrs Maxwell to join her in Washington. However, Mrs Maxwell reluctantly declined, as the Maxwells were in the process of opening a new Bahá'í centre in Montreal. She shared the details with Helen:

> *... a circular library of restful charm and interest, on a universal spiritual basis, with a background of finest thought in modern literature along lines entirely in harmony with the Bahá'í teachings: and by this means we hope to create as it were a spiritual and intellectual melting pot preparatory*

to the World Unity Conference to be held in the month of April.[31]

She then asked Helen to recommend a list of books:

... with your vision and touch on life. You have already mentioned a number of books to me in your letters, especially two or three books about the Negro race.[32]

In one of her most touching and emotional letters, Mrs Maxwell expressed her deep admiration and love for Helen:

Oh Helen! You remember the day Louis [Gregory] spoke at the home of Mrs. Kennedy and how the fire of love burning in your heart caused the clear drops of water to flow from your eyes. It was a lovely day, a marvelous atmosphere, Louis was like an angel, but you, My Helen, beautiful divine Helen, I can never forget your eyes under the shadow of your big hat, your firm cool, sweet, tender lips, your girlish grace, that beauty which is ineffable because it is of God.[33]

A few months later, in another letter to Helen, Mrs Maxwell hoped to see her during the Bahá'í Summer School at Green Acre, Maine:

There are many reasons why I earnestly hope that you may be in Green Acre this summer, the presence of Ruhi Effendi, the Board teaching plan, the Racial amity, standard of Unity, Horace [Holley], Mary [her daughter]. There is a world contained in each of these for your priceless gifts and rare spirit, and you are needed Helen, the Cause needs you at this juncture, and I believe new channels will be opened to you next winter through this vital contact now.[34]

A Change in Destiny

However, this anticipated reunion never came to pass. After graduating from high school, Helen planned to work and save money so that she could attend Green Acre Bahá'í School.

But providence had other plans.

In the summer of 1927, instead of travelling east to New England, Helen sailed west to Hawaii—on her honeymoon!

Marriage, College, and Pilgrimage

Helen's marriage came as a surprise to many of her friends. Upon hearing the news, May Maxwell wrote to her:

> *Your precious letter came the very day that I left Green Acre ... You must wonder at my silence since you wrote me of your marriage, but you are one of the very, very few who receive my silent message and always understand what I am thinking and feeling without the intermediary pen and paper*

... I confess I was stunned by your marriage, yet so like you in every way ... Tell your husband that I remember him in the Convention but I do not really know him well ... [35]

The groom, Charles Reed Bishop, came from a distinguished Hawaiian lineage. His grand-uncle and namesake, Charles Reed Bishop, was a pioneering American entrepreneur from New York who made Hawaiʻi his home, marrying Princess Beatrice Pauahi. He founded Hawaiʻi's first bank, and his wife, deeply devoted to her heritage, ensured that crown lands were preserved for the Hawaiian people. She was a passionate collector of Hawaiian artefacts, and after her passing, her husband established a museum in her honour. Today, the Charles Reed Museum houses the world's most extensive collection of Hawaiian and Pacific artefacts, along with natural history specimens.

Born on 24 October 1889, Charles was sixteen years older than Helen. His early years had been turbulent, marked by what Helen later described as "a brief but devastating marriage." However, in 1921, at the age of thirty, he underwent a profound transformation after encountering the teachings of Baháʼuʼlláh. Deeply moved, he embraced the Baháʼí Faith, embarked on a pilgrimage to the Holy Land, and met the beloved Guardian. That encounter solidified his resolve to dedicate his life to serving the Cause. Upon his return to Portland, he immersed himself in Baháʼí activities.

It was there, just months later, that he met Helen. Their connection was immediate—he fell deeply in love and soon asked her to be his wife.

A Marriage Rooted in Service

If Helen's marriage surprised May Maxwell, it evoked a different reaction from Louis Gregory. He wrote to her:

> *How happy indeed are 'Ye twain' to be so entirely one, linked together because of your love of the beauty of Truth and the Face of God both in time and eternity, great indeed is such a blessing and in this 'gloomy, disastrous age' so rare! Yet the fact that you are both youthful and are so well endowed with the spiritual gifts of the Master indicates that He has signalized for you great and increasing service to the human world.*[36]

His words proved prophetic. From the very beginning, Helen and Charles' marriage was built on love, mutual respect, and a shared devotion to service.

Charles deeply admired Helen's intellectual abilities and believed that the Bahá'í community needed teachers who were both spiritually and academically prepared. Fortunately, their home was near Reed College, a prestigious liberal arts institution. In 1928, Helen enrolled there as a freshman, embarking on her academic journey with a clear purpose—to better serve the Faith.

The moment she began college she sought guidance from the Guardian regarding the direction of her education. In response to one of her letters, Shoghi Effendi's secretary wrote on his behalf:

Because of his [the Guardian's] great desire to see young people active in teaching work ... he hopes that you will succeed in your studies and in due course add sound knowledge to your great desire for service.

Helen excelled in her studies, focusing on the social sciences and humanities. When the time came to write her senior thesis, she sought the Guardian's approval to centre her research on the Bahá'í Faith. His response was one of unwavering encouragement.

Her dissertation, The Rise and Diffusion of the Bahá'í Religion, examined the Faith through the lenses of sociology, anthropology, history, economics, and philosophy.

During her two-hour oral defence, professors probed her with challenging questions about this emerging religion. Helen's responses were eloquent and persuasive, earning her high academic distinction.

On completion of her college education, Shoghi Effendi encouraged her to expand her service

... beyond the confines of your own country.[37]

She later sent a copy of her thesis to him, and he not only praised her work but also expressed his hope that other Bahá'í students would

... follow the noble example you have set before them.[38]

The Influence of a Great Bahá'í Teacher

Helen's academic journey deepened her spiritual resolve. In 1930, while still in college, she had the extraordinary opportunity to meet Keith Ransom-Kehler, a renowned Bahá'í teacher and pioneer.

During her visit to Portland, Keith conducted public meetings, firesides, and study sessions for the Bahá'ís. Helen was profoundly inspired by her presence, recognising in her a model of dedication and clarity of purpose that she would cherish for the rest of her life.

Years later, she confided in her dear friend, Marion Holley, about Keith's impact on her spiritual growth:

> *When I had just embraced the Faith, I began to absorb the Teachings as I once had done novels. But the power to command ideas, to discriminate and construct—the 'masculine principle,' if you will—that was the legacy of Keith.* [39]

Meeting such a distinguished Bahá'í further ignited Helen's desire to serve with the same passion and energy as her mentor.

Thus, a new chapter of her spiritual journey was set in motion—one that the Guardian himself had envisioned for her.

Chapter 2

THE INTERNATIONAL BAHÁ'Í BUREAU

Chapter 2

The Cradle of the League of Nations

In the spring of 1925, the youthful Shoghi Effendi established the International Bahá'í Bureau in Geneva, the cradle of the League of Nations. Its purpose was to coordinate Bahá'í activities in Europe and to lay the groundwork for forming a spiritual assembly in the city.

Following the First World War, the victorious nations had chosen Geneva as the headquarters for the newly created League of Nations, transforming it into a diplomatic hub of the international community. The Bureau was initially managed by Mrs J Stannard, a well-known Bahá'í pioneer.

By June 1925, an office was acquired at 19 Boulevard Georges–Favon, furnished to accommodate its growing activities. Martha Root travelled to Geneva to assist with the Bureau's work, and through her efforts, the Esperanto Congress was held there in 1925 and 1926.

During these gatherings, Miss Lydia Zamenhof, daughter of Ludwig Zamenhof, the founder of Esperanto, attended the conferences. It was there that she first became interested in the Bahá'í Faith, later embracing its teachings and enrolling as a believer.

Challenges and Struggles : Keeping the Bureau Afloat

By autumn 1927, Mrs Stannard's failing health and financial difficulties made it impossible for her to continue managing the Bureau. In October, nine Bahá'ís gathered to consult on its future.

Although they knew how deeply the Guardian wished for the Bureau to remain operational, most of them believed that the financial obstacles were too great, and they voted to close the Bureau.

However, Miss Julia Culver, who had already travelled to Geneva to assist in the office, offered to take over responsibility for the Bureau—albeit with reduced activities.

In May 1928, she sought assistance from Mrs Emogene Hoagg, who, by June, had relocated from her pioneering post in Florence to Geneva. The Bureau's new headquarters were established at 20 Bis Rue Général-Dufour.

Shortly thereafter, the League of Nations formally recognised the Bahá'í Bureau, granting it membership in the *Fédération des Mouvements Internationaux*.

A Call to Service : Shoghi Effendi and the Bishops

By 1929, the Great Depression began to take its toll, creating organisational and financial difficulties for the Bureau. Shoghi Effendi, recognising the challenges it faced, reached out to Helen and Charles Bishop, asking if they would consider moving to Switzerland to assist with the work.

However, at that time, Helen was about to begin her college education, and Charles was experiencing financial setbacks. Regretfully, they had to decline. As Mrs Hoagg's health declined, the Bureau was maintained by two devoted staff members Miss Lentz, a German Bahá'í, and Mrs Lynch, a Russian Bahá'í.

In March 1931, the Guardian provided clarification on the status of the Bureau, stating:

> *Geneva is auxiliary to the Center in Haifa. It does not assume the place of Haifa, but is auxiliary. It exercises no international authority; it does not try to impose, but helps and acts as intermediary between Haifa and other Bahá'í centers. It is international because it links the different countries; it is like a distributing center.*[40]

In October 1932, Shoghi Effendi once again emphasised his belief that the Bishops were the most qualified Bahá'ís to lead the Bureau. He expressed these sentiments in a letter to Mrs Stuart W French, who promptly forwarded the letter to Helen and Charles.

The Bishops received it on 25 October—a day of profound significance.

A Sign from Providence

On the same day, they also received a cablegram announcing the tragic passing of Keith Ransom-Kehler. Just two nights earlier, on 23 October, Charles had an extraordinary dream. He described it to Helen:

> *The Guardian placed in my hand a scroll he had written for me. When I opened it, I found only one word: Keith.*

Within the next few months, they received three letters and a cablegram from Shoghi Effendi. One of these, dated the very same day that Charles had his dream, contained a message from the Guardian's secretary, written on his behalf to Helen:

> *You are the right person who is needed now that the [International Bahá'í] Bureau is acquiring an important international status in the Administration.*[41]

The Guardian's appeal was clear and direct.

By this time Helen had completed her college studies, and Charles' financial situation had improved. A key turning point came when Charles' paternal uncle, 'Uncle Faxon', president of C. Brenner & Co., reconsidered his previous reluctance toward Charles' Bahá'í commitments. In response to Charles' request, he authorised him to access his portion of the Bishop Trust funds.

With the financial barriers removed, the Bishops immediately accepted the call to serve.

Departure for Geneva : A Historic Journey

In January 1934, Helen and Charles left Portland, bound for the East Coast. Before taking up their post in Geneva, Shoghi Effendi invited them to the Holy Land.

On 14 February 1934—St Valentine's Day—they departed for Palestine aboard the ship Cotidi Savois. Among their fellow passengers were Chaim Weizmann, the future president of the State of Israel, and some 300 Jewish pilgrims travelling to the Tomb of Rachel.

With hearts filled with faith and determination, Helen and Charles set sail—knowing they were about to embark on one of the most significant chapters of their lives.

In the Presence of the Guardian

Three days before their departure from New York, Marion Holley wrote to Helen:

> *I am reminded that the hour comes when you will take yourself onto a boat and sail past the [Statue] of Liberty for the last time in no one knows how long. It is really such a tremendous move, not only from your standpoint, but from ours that my mind is really unable to understand it.*[42]

She was right. It was a journey that, to the end of her life, Helen considered the most magnificent spiritual experience she had ever had and the most precious and happiest period of her life.

Just before her pilgrimage, she wrote to Marion, recounting a dream:

> *In that dream, I went to Haifa with my husband and I heard him speak to me, gently admonishingly—because it was my turn to go into the Guardian's reception room and I faltered from awe and the sense of what I had left undone in the service of the Cause. The admonition was made when this strange and silent man to whom I was married, wished me to realize that while I was giving way to subjective reaction the Guardian was waiting. And waiting. I got myself together and entered a room filled with light. The Guardian stood between two Persians with superhuman height and these two Oriental figures stood before two gigantic windows giving a golden light. But when the light behind them converged upon the Guardian who stood between them, then I looked no*

more at them—but at the centered Light. And that was the Guardian.[43]

To Helen, for the rest of her life, the Guardian remained 'the centred Light.'

Meeting the Guardian

Helen promised Marion that she would share her impressions after her first meeting with Shoghi Effendi. Writing from Haifa, she described him vividly:

> *The Guardian rarely smiles or laughs, but when he does one would teach the Cause all around the world, and then die first for another brief moment of his pleasure.*[44]

Later, from Geneva, she wrote a more detailed account to Alfred Lunt:

> *It is a great experience to go to Haifa, and one's point of view changes on many matters. The Guardian is an example of how intellect can serve the spirit in a manner we in the west have never known. There is nothing emotional about the Guardian: he is the perfectly controlled and mature personality. I have never heard him recite an incident in which he was the major figure, or say anything which would in any way give him a chance to excel. This may sound naive but the point is that Shoghi Effendi simply refutes all those*

theories which our academics are surfeited: that every ego is trying merely to maximize itself.

Shoghi Effendi is very impersonal and he speaks only of the Word and the Faith. His speech is rapid and his English is stunning: when he speaks the hours pass tirelessly. I should say that his most obvious characteristic is power, but there is nothing arbitrary or even personal about it. Again and again he seems to convey that the Cause of Bahá'u'lláh will reach its aim and that we have only to be superlatively faithful and to be obedient and active. There is something about him that makes one to believe that we can do anything if he requires it: for example he tells me to write and I simply must begin to do it.

Shoghi Effendi says that the great world events will establish the Faith. It depends only partly upon the Bahá'ís. The war is inevitable and great changes will result therefrom ... The form of administration established in America will become form for the entire world.[45]

The days in the Holy Land passed quickly, and soon Helen had to turn her attention to the mission ahead of her in Geneva.

Transition of Leadership at the Bahá'í Bureau

When Helen took charge of the Bahá'í Bureau, it primarily served as an intermediary between Bahá'í assemblies, groups, and individuals in Europe and functioned as a centre for the distribution of information about the Faith.

Mrs Emogene Hoagg, who had tirelessly served the Faith in Europe, had to return to the United States for medical treatment. After a year, her health improved, and by the autumn of 1935, she inquired whether she should resume her work in Geneva. Shoghi Effendi, through his secretary Hussein Effendi Rabbani, advised her to

> ... remain in America and render her invaluable support to the urgent need of teaching in that country.[46]

Later, the Guardian requested that she go to Haifa to assist in typing the translation manuscript of *The Dawn-Breakers*.

Geneva Amidst Global Unrest

The Bishops arrived in Geneva in April 1934. For the world at large, it was a diplomatically chaotic time. What would become a decade of international anarchy began in 1931 when Japan invaded Manchuria, and no government showed any willingness to come to the support of the victim. The League of Nation's principle of 'collective security' was a dead letter. By 1934, Hitler had taken total control of the government in Germany, and he was about to renege on the international obligations to which Germany had agreed in signing the treaty of 1918. In Italy, fascism under Mussolini ruled supreme, and General Franco was about to bury the corpse of the republic in Spain. In the Soviet Union, Stalin was turning the state into a mechanism of absolute and pervasive repression.

The Guardian instructed Helen to travel and teach the Faith outside of Geneva, particularly in Germany, northern and central European countries, and in the Balkans. Before Hitler took over the German government, the progress of the Faith in that country seemed promising. The Cause was firmly established in Stuttgart and its surroundings (Esslingen, Göppingen, and Karlsruhe), and there were also solid Bahá'í groups in Frankfurt, Heidelberg, Hamburg, and Dresden. Germany had outstanding Bahá'í teachers such as Dr Hermann Grossman, Dr Adelbert Mühlschlegel, and Dr Eugene Schmidt, among others.

Continued Work in Germany and Austria

By 1935, Helen travelled extensively throughout Germany and played a key role in supporting local Bahá'í communities. In *The Bahá'í World: 1934-36*, a report describes her influence:

> *The Cause of German Bahá'ís has received great impetus through the presence of Mrs. Charles Bishop, who though stationed in Geneva, has made it possible to come to the Summer School, and also visit different groups throughout Germany, often accompanied by Miss Edith Horn who is now attached to the Frankfurt Branch ... Mrs. Bishop's great gift as a speaker illumines the hearts of her audience; the*

earnestness of her spirit and the charm of her personality make Helen Bishop an outstanding figure in the Bahá'í Cause and a most welcome guest at every gathering.[47]

By late 1936, the Bahá'í School at Esslingen reached its peak, drawing Bahá'ís from Iran, England, America, and Scandinavia. Heidelberg hosted what would be the last annual Bahá'í convention in Germany before Heinrich Himmler banned Bahá'í institutions. In a special report, Dr and Mrs Grossmann and his sister spoke of their pilgrimage to Haifa. Mark Tobey, the renowned American painter who was pioneering in England at the time, represented the National Assembly of Great Britain at the convention, receiving an enthusiastic welcome. Before their departure for the Holy Land on 25 December, May Maxwell and her daughter, Mary, visited Bahá'ís in both the north and south of Germany, as did Agnes Alexander and Madame Barry-Orlova.

In Austria, too, before the German takeover, the Faith showed promising growth. In the summer of 1936, the Wiener Journal, a well-known Viennese newspaper, published an article titled *Viennese Spread Persian Religion*, featuring the Bahá'í teachings. That same year, the Esperanto Congress convened in Vienna, where Lydia Zamenhof organised a special session on the Bahá'í Faith and delivered a lecture on the Revelation of Bahá'u'lláh.

Facing Nazi Oppression

As the Nazi grip tightened across Germany, it became increasingly difficult for Bahá'ís to maintain their activities. Helen's public lectures were required to have an 'official hearer,' a Gestapo agent who monitored her words. In Frankfurt, authorities ordered the cancellation of her talk when she refused to sign an 'artikel' that would have barred non-Aryans from attending. The Guardian reassured her in a letter:

> *The more the obstacles develop in strength and number, the firmer your faith shall become in the sacredness and vital importance of the mission you have been called upon to fulfill for the Cause in Germany.*[48]

Helen later recalled in a letter to a friend that, during her farewell visit to the Guardian in Haifa, he had asked her:

> *Are you a patient person?*

She admitted: 'No, my beloved Guardian, unfortunately that is not one of my virtues.'

To this, Shoghi Effendi had simply replied:

> *I am sending you to Geneva to learn patience.*[49]

Her mission in Europe during those tumultuous years tested her resilience. The challenge was not only external, facing repressive governments that sought to suppress the Bahá'í Faith, but also internal—dealing with new Bahá'ís who had not yet fully grasped the principles of Bahá'u'lláh's New World Order. Some struggled to adapt to the Administrative Order, and a few even questioned why a woman—and an American—held such confidence from the Guardian and was entrusted with teaching the Faith across Germany. Fortunately, such sentiments were rare, and Helen was warmly welcomed by the majority of Bahá'ís, both in Germany and England.

The Ban on Bahá'í Institutions

By the end of 1936, Nazi authorities had effectively halted all Bahá'í activities in Germany. On 9 June 1937, the German government officially dissolved the National Spiritual Assembly of Germany/Austria. Austria followed soon after, issuing an order on 1 July 1937 banning all Bahá'í institutions and meetings.

Helen's report, *Geneva Scans the European Community*, reflected the grim reality:

> As the totalitarian states in Europe do not allow circulation of spiritual concepts regarding World Commonwealth, Bahá'í activities is wanting in many countries.[50]

Despite the suppression in Germany and Austria, Bahá'í activities continued in other European countries, and Helen's account remains a valuable historical source on the Faith's progress during this period.

Challenges in Geneva

Charles Bishop, the quiet and gentle intellectual, never felt at home in Geneva. The city's oppressive political climate clashed with his temperament, and he found the slow growth of the Faith, combined with internal disputes among some Bahá'ís, frustrating. Almost immediately after arriving in Europe, he returned to the United States, but after some time, he returned to Geneva to support Helen in her work.

The Guardian expressed his concern for Charles in a letter to Helen, reassuring her that he was praying for him and encouraging him to persevere, and hoping that he 'would soon adjust himself to [the] Geneva milieu' and will no more feel 'restless and impatient.'[51]

In another letter, Shoghi Effendi urged Charles to take a more active role in Bahá'í activities. Shoghi Effendi expressed the hope that

> ... he will feel fit to assist you in your important mission of promoting and consolidating the Cause throughout Europe.[52]

Charles, however, remained restless and disconnected from Geneva's Bahá'í work. Helen, in contrast, continued her efforts, expanding the Bureau's influence and engaging with European Bahá'ís as tensions mounted across the continent.

Strengthening the Faith in Britain

With the dissolution of the German/Austrian National Spiritual Assembly, only one Bahá'í national institution remained on the European continent—Great Britain.

In February 1936, the British National Spiritual Assembly, with Shoghi Effendi's approval, invited Helen and Charles to assist the National Teaching Committee in developing a new teaching program. Upon arriving in London, Helen was immediately scheduled for public talks. She conducted firesides at Lady Blomfield's home and led weekly classes on the Dispensation of Bahá'u'lláh at Mrs George's residence.

To strengthen communication between Bahá'ís across Britain, Helen worked closely with David Hofman to establish the Teaching Bulletin, a publication designed to:

- Keep isolated Bahá'ís connected to national community life
- Circulate important messages from the Guardian
- Encourage greater participation in teaching efforts

By April 1936, Helen and Charles travelled to Devonshire and Torquay, where they met Mark Tobey, the pioneering American painter who had settled in England. Helen delivered a lecture at Dartington Hall, where Tobey taught painting.

She was also invited to speak at a Theosophical Society gathering and a Practical Psychology Centre event. Both audiences were receptive to her presentations on the Bahá'í Faith, and her presence helped establish connections between the British Baháʼí community and wider intellectual circles.

The World Congress of Faiths

The second International Fellowship of The World Congress of Faiths took place in London over two weeks in July 1936. From 3–17 July, daily sessions were held at the Great Hall of London University, with four public meetings convened at Queen's Hall. The central theme of the Congress was 'World Fellowship Through Religion.'

Helen described the event as

> *a representative gathering of religionists, liberal and free-thinkers, scientists and philosophers—and thus a temptation to doctrinal debate or interplay of minds—but its intention was thoroughly practical.*[53]

The organiser of the Congress was Sir Francis Younghusband, a British Army officer, explorer, and spiritual writer, who served as the British National Chairman of the World Fellowship. Sir Francis personally wrote to Shoghi Effendi, inviting him to attend and participate in the Congress. The event itself was chaired by Sir Herbert Samuel, later Viscount Samuel of Carmel, who had been the first High Commissioner for Palestine under the British Mandate.

Sir Herbert was well acquainted with the Bahá'í Faith, an admirer of 'Abdu'l-Bahá, and was eager for Shoghi Effendi to be present at the gathering.

Shoghi Effendi's Response

Due to his heavy commitments, Shoghi Effendi was unable to attend or prepare a paper for the occasion. Instead, he asked the National Spiritual Assembly of Great Britain to represent him at the Congress.

His secretary also wrote on his behalf to George Townshend, who was still officially the Archdeacon of the Church of Ireland, requesting that he present the Faith at the event.

Archdeacon Townshend had met 'Abdu'l-Bahá in 1911 in England and had long been deeply drawn to the Bahá'í teachings. He recognised Bahá'u'lláh as the return of the Father, though he had not yet publicly declared this from the pulpit. While he had not officially severed ties with the Church of Ireland, his sermons often reflected the Bahá'í Message, presenting it as the modern realisation of Christ's teachings.

At one point, in 1928, he had even considered accepting the directorship of the International Bahá'í Bureau in Geneva while remaining a clergyman. David Hofman, in his biography of Townshend, described the tension he faced:

> *[In Geneva] where he saw Emogene Hoagg and other Bahá'ís giving their full energies to Bahá'í service, made*

a deep impression on him ... Life in Ahascragh [village in Ireland] could offer nothing of the excitement of the international atmosphere of Geneva and certainly none of the companionship of the Bahá'ís.[54]

The archdeacon had rendered

... prodigious services to the Guardian in relation to the translations of **The Kitab-i Iqan, Nabil's Narrative, Gleanings From the Writings of Bahá'u'lláh,** *and* **Prayers and Meditations of Bahá'u'lláh.**[55]

There can be no doubt that the perusal of the three volumes of the sacred texts of the new Revelation and the heroic saga of *The Dawn-Breakers* profoundly influenced his mind and heart. He reached such a deeper understanding of the claims and mission of Bahá'u'lláh that on 23 April 1933, he was impelled to write to the Guardian:

I trust and pray that very soon God will release me from my clerical position and permit me to serve His Cause openly, and do nothing else. I am ready now to go anywhere and do anything for Bahá'u'lláh.[56]

Townshend's Pivotal Decision

By inviting Townshend to present the Bahá'í Faith at the London Congress, Shoghi Effendi was offering him the opportunity to formally part ways with his clerical role.

The Guardian's letter to him was dated 9 December 1935, and Townshend received it on 20 December. Within an hour, he responded:

> *My heart is charged with gratitude to God for thus giving me the opportunity which recently I have been planning to make in some way myself. I will write that paper and will go to London and read it myself: and the power of the All Merciful will be with me to convince and to move. My heart's thanks to you … The fact that a clergyman (and worse still an archdeacon) presents this argument [the coming of the Kingdom of God on earth] will itself cause immense comment and criticism. That is what the emergency needs. My position in the Church will quickly become untenable, of course, but you will understand that this will cause me no spiritual sorrow.* [57]

Shoghi Effendi was deeply moved by Townshend's resolve and wrote back:

> *I truly admire, and am deeply touched by the tone of your response to my request. Your courage and determination in the face of the developments that may ensue as a result of your resolve to read the paper are worthy of the highest praise. Bahá'u'lláh will no doubt be watching you and make you victorious. For you and your dear wife, who will share with you the glory which such an action must someday bring you, I shall pray from the bottom of my heart, rest assured and persevere.* [58]

Helen's Role in the Congress

Shoghi Effendi also asked Helen to represent the Bahá'í Faith from the perspective of the International Bahá'í Bureau in Geneva.

When Helen and Charles arrived in England, Dr Townshend welcomed them warmly, sending them a letter that reflected both his enthusiasm and his challenges:

> *I am delighted to hear you are in England spreading the good news, and I wish we could ask you to this distressful country [Ahsacragh, his own diocese] to do the same. But the time is not ripe; except for this household I know of only one single believer and only of one sympathizer (a half-sister) in the whole four provinces ... Do write me when you have time and tell me fully your impression of England and the Message: are they getting ready for it?*[59]

In the same letter, he also referenced the upcoming Congress in London and confessed his difficult position:

> *... I could only accept the privilege the Guardian offered me on the express condition that I could not say anything in direct violation of my ordination vows and that my paper could not be official.*[60]

Yet, despite this internal struggle, Townshend recognised the greater purpose behind his actions. His final words in the letter to Helen revealed his deep commitment to the Faith:

*I have given ... an order for the new edition of **The Promise of All Ages**, giving the true name of the author to be ready for delivery before the end of June. This, with my appearance speaking on the platform on the Bahá'í Cause, will inevitably bring the Church of England and the Church of Ireland, backed by the Church tenets, in the fray. Therefore this seems to me the best way of making the utmost use of the opportunity, and we will get the Cause ablazed abroad by the Enemy as well as by our Friends. All this is the last development I ever looked for, and the last for which I feel personally fitted. It is God's will. I certainly am not going to run away now ... Yours in His Name. George Townshend.*[61]

The Bahá'í Session at the World Congress of Faiths

The Bahá'í session at the World Congress of Faiths was held on the morning of 16 July 1936, chaired by Sir Herbert Samuel. In his opening remarks, he made a striking statement about the Bahá'í Faith's unique role in fostering world unity:

If one were compelled to choose which of the many communities of the world was closest to the aim and purpose of this Congress, I think one would be obliged to say it was the comparatively little known Bahá'í community. Other faiths and creeds have to consider, at a congress like this, in what way they can contribute to the idea of world fellowship. But the Bahá'í Faith exists almost for the sole purpose of contributing to the fellowship and the unity of mankind.

Other communities may consider how far a particular element of their faith may be regarded as similar to those of other communities, but the Bahá'í Faith exists for the purpose of combining in one synthesis all those elements in the various faiths which are held in common. And that is why I suggest that this Bahá'í community is really more in agreement with the main idea which has held the summoning of the Congress than any particular one of the great religious communities of the world. [62]

Dr George Townshend's address to the Congress was both eloquent and profound. He boldly declared that the 'Father' had returned:

The Ground Plan of World Fellowship which is now submitted to your consideration was composed out of the Writings of Bahá'u'lláh and presented by 'Abdu'l-Bahá in London, and later in Paris about a quarter of a century ago ...

Intellectual vision never was so keen as in this generation; but spiritual vision, was it ever so weak? We talk, we boast of a New Age, but we miss its greatest gift. We say that the human race is at last reaching maturity, but we do not realize the fullness, the completeness of this growth ...

Bahá'u'lláh clearly affirms that without spirituality, a loftier and firmer faith in the Universal Father, mankind will not discover the way out of its troubles ... no difficulty, no delay, no defeat which may take shape as we advance can even stem the onward march of Heaven's purpose, that within man's soul are ample powers to win all that we desire, and the banner under which mankind will stand at last united is that spiritual faith in love of Almighty God, which is the universal heritage of all of us.[63]

Following Dr Townshend's address, the chairman introduced Helen, referring to her as 'Mrs Charles Bishop', and invited her to represent the International Bahá'í Bureau.

Helen's speech was concise but deeply insightful, focusing on Persia's spiritual contributions to the world. She highlighted how three great religious movements had emerged from Persia—Zoroastrianism, the Bábí Faith, and the Bahá'í Faith:

The illustrious Ancestor of the Báb was the Prophet Muhammad and Bahá'u'lláh is descended from the ancient Zoroastrian kings. And so we have in the Bahá'í Faith the appearance of the two great branches of religion. By this alliance, an old family feud is abolished: we have an historic basis for reconciliation and fellowship.[64]

She concluded her speech by quoting from Shoghi Effendi's The Goal of a New World Order, describing the Bahá'í vision for a united world:

… Such indeed appears, in its broadest outline, the Order anticipated by Bahá'u'lláh, an Order that shall come to be regarded as the fairest fruit of a slowly maturing age.[65]

The Guardian's Response to Townshend's Historic Stand

That same afternoon, Dr Townshend wrote directly to Shoghi Effendi, reporting the success of the Bahá'í session:

> *This morning the Bahá'í paper, 'The Ground Plan of World Fellowship,' was read ... by an Irish clergyman, and was received without any dissenting voice ... Miss Sharples, the chief secretary of the Society that is behind the Congress told me later in the day that everybody in the hall felt the unifying influence of the paper. Sir Samuel Herbert was in the chair and stated he knew no movement which concentrated its efforts as much on the promotion of world fellowship. So — that is that. I regard this as the end of my clerical career and, if God permit, the opening of a more useful life of service to the Cause of Bahá'u'lláh. Soon authorities will ask me for explanation and for apologies which I shall be unable to give. I have no idea what shape things will take. I am just in the hands of God. There is no more to say. I am loyally yours in His service ...* [66]

Shoghi Effendi responded immediately, expressing his admiration for Townshend's courage:

> *Your heroic determination to face the consequences of your fearless act on behalf of our beloved Cause has touched my heart and enhanced my admiration for what you have already achieved in the service of His Faith. I will pray for your guidance, strength and success. You will no doubt be*

> *reinforced by the hosts of the Abha Kingdom. The Beloved is well-pleased with the spirit that animates you.*[67]

That July day marked a turning point—the Church of Ireland lost an archdeacon, but the Cause of Bahá'u'lláh gained a fearless champion. In 1953, George Townshend was among the first twelve Hands of the Cause of God appointed by Shoghi Effendi.

Helen's Role in Documenting the Congress

Helen later sent a detailed report on the Congress to Shoghi Effendi. Two days after responding to Dr Townshend, the Guardian wrote to Helen, thanking her for her insightful and thorough account. In his own handwriting, he added:

> *I know no one better qualified to write such an interesting report for The Bahá'í World.*[68]

Helen's 'Report on London Congress' was subsequently published in *The Bahá'í World: 1936-38*.

Public Teaching Efforts in England

The National Teaching Committee had made meticulous plans for Helen's lectures. They hoped that, with her and Charles' assistance, a Spiritual Assembly could be formed in Torquay, where Mark Tobey was pioneering and a Bahá'í group already existed.

On 3 January 1937, Dr Tudor-Jones, a Unitarian Minister who had met 'Abdu'l-Bahá in 1911, offered his pulpit to Helen. From that platform, she proclaimed the coming of the Lord of the Ages.

Three weeks later, she returned to deliver another talk, titled 'Do You Know in What Age You Live?'

Helen also spoke at the South Devonshire Literary and Debating Society and twice at the Theosophical Society. While her audiences responded enthusiastically, few were ready to commit to the Bahá'í Faith.

The following month, while in London, Helen developed severe bronchitis. On her doctor's recommendation, she returned to Torquay for rest. She cabled Dr Mühlschlegel for medical advice, and he sent her homeopathic tablets.

Years later, in a 1951 personal note reviewing her medical history, Helen recalled:

> ... a wise and venerable Persian cabled the Guardian, Shoghi Effendi, at Mount Carmel. His prayers were heard and I recovered.[69]

The Marriage of Shoghi Effendi

In March 1937, the Bishops were in London when the British National Assembly received a momentous cablegram:

Announce Assemblies celebration marriage beloved Guardian. Imperishable honor upon the handmaid of Bahá'u'lláh, Rúḥíyyih Khánum, Miss Mary Maxwell. Ziya'iyyih. Mother of the Guardian.[70]

For Bahá'ís around the world, the news brought great joy. David Hofman, then Secretary of the National Spiritual Assembly of the British Isles, reflected on its profound significance:

The union of the East and the West, so dear to the Master's heart, has been cemented in His own family.[71]

Helen, a close friend of the Maxwells for over a decade, immediately sent a heartfelt letter of congratulations to Rúḥíyyih Khánum, along with a wedding gift.

Shortly after, Rúḥíyyih Khánum responded in her own handwriting:

My dear Helen, your kind letter added to my happiness which is already complete with this infinite bounty of Bahá'u'lláh. We often feel through our Faith and love that we have granted a little of the meaning of God's love and bounty. But He has vouchsaved me such a share that I can only bow before His mystery and confess 'the ways of God are not always of men,' and that He bestows regardless of merit or worthiness. I feel in my heart that you know how overwhelming such a thing is.

It was most kind of you to suggest doing my shopping I might need and I would not hesitate to take advantage of your help, knowing what excellent taste you have! But at present there is really nothing to be done. Please give Charles my warm greetings. I feel so close to you who are such devoted and ever sacrificing servant of our most Precious Cause.

Lovingly, Ruhiyyih [72]

A Second Letter of Gratitude

Two weeks later, Helen received another personal note from the bride, again written in her own hand:

My dear Helen, your charming gift, as usual breathing your excellent good taste, delighted me. Thank you so much for it ... I think it is a lovely gift for this occasion, but then as I know how close you and Charles are to the Guardian and how all your ceaseless service, which I love and admire you forever so much, has drawn you ever closer to him ... How precious every capacity we have is when we are giving our all to the Faith. If the Cause only had more like you.

Lovingly, Ruhiyyih [73]

It is interesting to note that two years before the Guardian's marriage, in January 1935, when Helen sent her annual report on the International Bahá'í Bureau to Shoghi Effendi, she enclosed a cheque for $300, imploring him to spend it on himself.

In his reply dated 1 February 1935, the Guardian expressed his gratitude but informed her that her contribution would instead be used for the construction of the Shrine of the Báb.

Reflections from Bahá'í Friends

From California, Helen received a letter from Marion Holley—the future Mrs Hofman—who shared her own sense of awe at the significance of this moment:

> *I thought of you a hundred times since the news of the Guardian's marriage reached us. What I would give to share the reverberation of spirit, which this earth-shaking event has caused ... I am confident that the Faith will be vitalized ... that a new phase of accomplishment is fast approaching ... these are days which will resound throughout all the history of our planet. The unity of the East and the West is cemented.*[74]

In another letter, Marion observed the immense responsibility that Rúḥíyyih Khánum now carried:

> *Despite herself and her natural gifts [Mary's] actions too [are] bound to elevate toward, not to, this same plane. Hers*

is a superhuman task: yet no one does expect she will fail. I look for transformation of a miraculous sort, a refinement of perception, a steadiness of conduct, a dependability which is not of herself but by will of God.[75]

In Praise of Words

While Helen was recuperating in Torquay, Shoghi Effendi asked her to draft an article for the forthcoming edition of The Bahá'í World. Though honoured by the request, she found it a daunting task.

Two years earlier, the Guardian had translated into English *Gleanings from the Writings of Bahá'u'lláh*, a work that deeply moved Helen. It made her reflect on the power of divine words, yet she did not relish the idea of putting her thoughts on paper. Writing was not her preferred mode of expression; she was a gifted platform speaker, known for her eloquence and compelling presence.

Honor Kempton, herself a renowned speaker, once wrote to Helen, admiring her unique combination of 'beauty, grace, spirit and intellect'[76] and that she used those qualities 'generously to teach the Cause of God.'[77]

Similarly, in 1940, while pioneering in Salt Lake City, Marguerite Sears shared a letter with Helen in which her father, a dedicated and discerning Bahá'í, praised her speaking abilities:

> My father wrote glowingly of your talk in Green Bay and went so far as to place you at the top of the speakers that he had heard so far. That seems to me to be a fine report; my father is very critical. He is so devoted to the Cause that he always wants for it the best.[78]

Yet now, the Guardian was not asking her to speak—he was asking her to write. Obedience to Shoghi Effendi left her no choice.

The Challenge of Writing

Though reluctant, Helen began composing her reflections on Bahá'u'lláh's Writings, ultimately titling her article 'In Praise of Words.'

When she sent the finished piece to Shoghi Effendi, she enclosed a letter expressing her inner struggle with the writing process:

> I hope that it will be acceptable to you because I anguish over every word. Francis Bacon said, 'speaking will bring forth a brilliant man, but writing an exact man.' When I confront an audience, words come and then flow from me, but when I take a pen, the words do not come easily or please me either.[79]

Yet, despite her hesitations, Helen's written voice proved just as elegant and precise as her spoken one. The opening paragraph of 'In Praise of Words' defined its central theme:

> *It is not the romance of the words which we praise, nor do we hold a brief for those philosophers who by lure of words have seduced minds from the realities of the common sense. We do find it timely to call an inquest for theologies that have obscured the meaning of words, terms, and figures, and thereby withheld followers from the recognition of God through His Prophets. This is the end that we exalt above all others: the Words of God enunciated by the Prophets, now again sent forth as entities charged with such '...potency as can instill new life into every human frame.'*[80]

From beginning to end, Helen crafted her article with a clear and direct message, deeply rooted in Bahá'u'lláh's teachings:

> *The words of Bahá'u'lláh are Logos and constitute a collective force of the first order, which by power of Spirit consciously and unconsciously subdues the mind, informs and recreates them in Truth. This world is the descent into existence; the Manifestation offers the ascent into being: here we are born into time; the Manifestation gives the rebirth into eternity. The Words of God draws the souls of men to life eternal; men, seeking a foretaste of that immortality, strive to perpetuate themselves on earth as well as by carving their names into history ...*

Bahá'u'lláh leads us into a commonwealth of Nations, which is more than an expansion and association; for the Divine Polity takes the nations into another dimension which searches the base and reaches the height of unity. We are called upon to be the citizens of Heaven and of 'Thy Kingdom on earth': world government lies within the power of the creative Word.[81]

This article, though outside Helen's natural comfort zone, became one of her most widely read writings, reinforcing her reputation as not just a dynamic speaker but also a compelling writer.

Farewell to Europe

As Helen wrote about the joy of the birth of a New World Order, the old one was already collapsing. Europe was moving towards destruction, its political climate darkening with the rise of authoritarianism.

From the moment the Bishops moved to Europe, Charles never felt at home. He found the oppressive atmosphere intolerable and struggled with the weight of an impending conflict. By 1 June 1937, Helen wrote to Shoghi Effendi, informing him of her husband's decision to return to the United States permanently that summer. She was torn—she wished to continue her teaching work for a while longer in Europe before reuniting with Charles in the autumn.

Shoghi Effendi received the news with deep regret. His secretary, writing on his behalf, expressed his feelings:

> *[He] deplores this quite sudden and unexpected turning point in the career of your international services to the Faith. The sacrifices you have so patiently born during these years have been truly marvelous ... and are remembered with deepest gratitude and appreciation by our beloved Guardian.*[82]

Helen was faced with an agonising choice. She had devoted herself entirely to the Guardian's request—to teach the Faith in Europe—but she could not abandon her faithful and loving husband either.

Final Months

After Charles' departure, Helen remained in Great Britain until 30 October. In September, she travelled to Manchester for two weeks, delivering daily public lectures and conducting firesides. Her efforts had a significant impact, leading to a marked increase in attendance at the Bahá'í Centre in Commerce Hall.

Returning to London in October, she received an invitation from Lady Blomfield to speak at a special session of the prestigious Near and Middle Eastern Association, which Lady Blomfield had personally arranged. Helen's speech left a lasting impression on the distinguished audience. The Association's secretary, HW Boffin, expressed his admiration in a letter to Lady Blomfield:

Mrs. Bishop is an able and convincing speaker. I was much impressed by the lucid simplicity with which she spoke, the impression that she gave that her words were chosen with great care to express exactly the meaning she intended to give.[83]

Two days later, he wrote directly to Helen, sharing how profoundly her words had resonated with him:

I feel I really must thank you for your address on Monday last at Lady Blomfield's house ... You have a great message to deliver. Mankind seems in these days to be caught in a terrible net of hate, fear, and misunderstanding. The appalling result is only too easy to foresee. I am one of those who believes that the work to dissipate this nightmare of illusions must come from the invisible, as I call it, from the spiritual plane, that is to say, working outward into the material. I mention this because it will show you why I found your address particularly helpful and inspiring, given as it was with lucid simplicity that I thought was most impressive.[84]

Helen was deeply moved by the response to her final weeks of teaching, but the time had come to depart Europe.

A Final Letter to the Guardian

On 30 October 1937, Helen stood in Southampton, ready to board the passenger ship back to the United States. Before doing so, she wrote one last letter to Shoghi Effendi. She expressed her sorrow at leaving Europe—the place where she had devoted years of tireless service—but also acknowledged that she had no other choice.

The Guardian's reply was filled with both sadness and encouragement. Through his secretary, he assured Helen:

> *He can not but deeply grieve over your departure from Europe ... where you have accomplished during those years services that are truly unforgettable and worthy of every consideration and praise ... However, it is not so much the place where one works that matters. The essential is the quality of the work one is able to attain ... The experience you have gathered in both teaching and the administrative sphere of Bahá'í work on the Continent are tremendous assets in your future area of service. In America friends will rejoice in your return and surely will benefit from the presence in their midst of such a devoted and loyal teacher as you.*[85]

For the time being, Shoghi Effendi appointed Mrs Lynch as the new Director of the International Bahá'í Bureau.

Helen's chapter in Europe had closed, but her work for the Faith was far from over. A new journey awaited her in America.

Photos

Bishop siblings in Mazatlan, c. 1910
Left to right: Gladys, Bobby, Helen, Jack.

Father, Portland 1918

Diamond Head, Hawaii, 1927
Helen and her mother.

Enhanced Photos

On boat to Hawaii for honeymoon, c. 1928

Geyserville Baha'i School, CA, 1928-9

Left to right: Kera Munson, Honor Kempton, Captain Marshall, Helen Bishop.

Honor Kempton, English Baha'i who was an early pioneer to Alaska after Shoghi Effendi's 1939 appeal for Baha'is to settle in every state of the United States. She later was one of the first Baha'I pioneers to settle in Luxembourg, arriving there in 1946.

Under the big tree at Geyserville Baha'i school, CA, 1930
Left to right: John Quinn, Helen Bishop, Marion Holley (4th from left), John Bosch, Arthur Dahl (standing), Dr Mildred Nichols, Evelyn Kemp, Charles Bishop.

Wilmette, IL, 1933, Temple meeting

Orcella Rexford (Gregory), the woman from whom Helen Bishop first heard the Baha'i message is second from the left. Charles is front row, sixth from the left. Sylvia Ioas is third from the left. Leroy Ioas, later a Hand of the Cause, is to her right, behind her.

Helen in Germany, c.1935

Baha'i summer school, Esslingen, Germany, 1936

May Maxwell, later Ruhiyyih Khanum, in front row, second from the right (next to the bush); Horace Holley, back row, sixth from the left; George Latimer, back row, seventh from the left.

Charles and George Townsend, England, 1936
(future Hand of the Cause)

London, 1937

Helen seated in the back; David Hofman, future member of the Universal House of Justice on the left; Hasan Balyuzi on the lower right.

Enhanced Photos

England Summer School, Derbyshire, UK, 1937
Helen, second row middle; Hasan Balyuzi in front row below her; Mark Tobey, American painter and pioneer to the UK, back row, first on the right.

Louhelen Baha'i School, Louhelen, MI, August, 1939

Helen with walking with students from her class.

Enhanced Photos

First Latin American Baha'i session,
Temerity Ranch, Pine Valley, Colorado Springs, CO, 1940
Helen Bishop front row, right; Charles Bishop, back row.

Geyserville, CA, c. July, 1940
John and Louise Bosch, Adrian Ellis in the middle.

Japan, c. 1950s
Charles Bishop and Hand of the Cause Agnes Alexander. The Bishops were travel-teaching in East Asia.

Wilmette IL, c. 1950s
Horace Holley, Doris Holley (to his left), and "Mrs Stee..." (to his right).

Boise, Idaho, 1953
Hand of the Cause Tarazu'llah Samandari
visits the Bishops (right).

Chapter 3

RETURN TO AMERICA

Chapter 3

The Seven Year Plan

After three years abroad, Helen returned to a homeland that had changed significantly. When she and Charles left the United States in 1933, the nation was deep in the greatest economic depression in its history. With a quarter of the labour force unemployed, despair hung in the air. Franklin Roosevelt, newly elected the year before, had promised a 'New Deal' for economic recovery and social reform. His first 100 days in office demonstrated a determination to bring about rapid and sweeping change.

By the time Helen arrived in New York three years later, the New Deal had not fully resolved the economic crisis—unemployment remained high—but a shift in national mood was undeniable. Signs of economic recovery gave Americans a renewed sense of self-reliance and optimism. Roosevelt's overwhelming re-election in 1936 reinforced public faith in his leadership. His second '100 days' in office were nearly as transformative as his first.

However, as the New World emerged from the depths of the Great Depression, the Old World of Europe spiralled deeper into fear, hatred, and violence.

A World on the Brink of War

By 1936, Europe was preparing for self-destruction. A 'cult of violence' dictated international affairs, and global anarchy spread unchecked. That year, Hitler's troops crossed into the Rhineland, violating both the Treaty of Versailles and the Treaty of Locarno. Yet, the League of Nations did nothing. Woodrow Wilson's principle of collective security, the foundation of the League, had effectively become a dead letter.

That July, General Franco launched a fascist rebellion in Spain, backed by Hitler and Mussolini. Yet, the League of Nations implemented a 'non-intervention' policy, effectively sealing the fate of Spain's democratic government. Meanwhile, in the United States, isolationist sentiment prevailed—Congress passed a new 'Neutrality Act', barring military support to any side in civil or international wars.

By October 1936, Germany and Italy formalised their alliance, dividing Eastern Europe and the Mediterranean as their spheres of expansion. Japan soon joined, and by November, the Rome-Berlin-Tokyo Axis was formed, cementing a global fascist bloc.

Against this ominous backdrop, Helen set her focus on the great challenge the Guardian had placed before the American Bahá'í community—the Seven Year Plan.

A Historic Call to Action

The Seven Year Plan of 1937 was the first of Shoghi Effendi's systematic global expansion strategies. As Ali Nakhjavani described:

> *The Bahá'í world entered the second Bahá'í century with the proud knowledge that the first epoch of the Formative Age had terminated, that the light of Bahá'u'lláh's teachings had now reached nearly eighty countries, that the Bahá'í community had achieved a major step in the construction of the Mother Temple of the West, and that this community was now ready to further extend the range of its institutions and consolidate its administrative structure. Shoghi Effendi had been patiently and systematically educating and preparing the Bahá'í world for the implementation of the two broad objectives he had in mind for his unique ministry. The first was **to strengthen the foundations of the structure of the Administrative Order**, both locally and nationally, so that it could sustain the weight of the dome of that structure which he repeatedly identified in The Ten Year Crusade in his letters, in English and in Persian, as the Universal House of Justice. The second broad objective was **to train the nascent institutions of the Faith in the concept of collective action** aimed at executing step-by-step each and every wish expressed by 'Abdu'l-Bahá in the Tablets of the Divine Plan.*[86]

The Guardian called upon the North American Bahá'í community to form at least one spiritual assembly in every state of the union and every province of Canada by 1944, the year of the Centennial

Celebration of the Báb's Declaration of His Mission. The Plan also anticipated, among other goals, the completion of the external structure of the House of Worship in Wilmette, for which 'Abdu'l-Bahá himself had set the foundation stone in 1912. The Guardian, in addition, challenged American Bahá'ís with objectives beyond their own borders: establishing a permanent centre of the Faith in each of the republics of Central and South America.

The enormity of the goals for that blessed but small community can only be measured by the fact that in 1937, after having been introduced to the Americas 43 years earlier, the Bahá'í community had only been able to form seventy-two local assemblies in twenty-six states and Canadian provinces, and there were about twenty-four Bahá'í groups—which amounted to fewer than nine individuals in a township—and 246 isolated believers.

Despite these limitations, the Guardian challenged the American believers not only to expand their community but also to confront one of the nation's most deep-seated social ills—racial prejudice.

A Call for Racial Unity

In 1937, the same year he launched the Seven Year Plan, Shoghi Effendi penned *The Advent of Divine Justice*, in which he warned the American Bahá'ís that the most challenging issue facing the United States was racism, and its eradication was necessary for the country's cultural, political, and spiritual survival.

The Guardian made it clear: expanding the Bahá'í Faith in America could not be separated from the struggle against racial prejudice. Responding to his call, the National Spiritual Assembly of North America urged every Bahá'í assembly to hold public meetings in January 1938, focusing on the oneness of humanity and the abolition of racism. On 21 December, they reissued the appeal, calling for nationwide action.

A New Life in America

Upon returning to the United States, the Bishops did not seek to 'settle down'. Instead, they prioritised mobility—the ability to travel freely and support the Plan's teaching efforts.

They decided to stay in Geyserville, California, at the Bahá'í summer school, founded on land donated by John and Louise Bosch.

From the very start, Helen's greatest wish was to pioneer in Latin America, as the Guardian had encouraged her to do. But Charles did not share the same desire. Helen confided in a Bahá'í friend in Vancouver:

> *By all the rules of common sense, I ought to go somewhere in Spanish-America—but I cannot get there to stay forever without being a bad wife to my good Bahá'í partner. Of that I shall say no more.*[87]

Charles had struggled in Europe and was even less inclined to move to Latin America. To Marion Holley, Helen admitted that he does not want

> ... to live again in the blackness of not knowing the language. Nor does he feel a call within himself to learn.[88]

To Mark Tobey, who knew and loved Charles, Helen was even more direct:

> Let those go who have not as yet tried to pioneer.[89]

Helen faced a dilemma—she was a wife, but also a devoted servant of the Guardian's Plan. In another letter to Marion Holley, she revealed her inner turmoil:

> ... the Guardian told me to go home and make Charles happy. That I am trying to do. Honor [Kempton] urged me to go to South America. So do you ... I believe in my own destiny, but I am not persuaded that my destiny is what I want it to be. Bahá'u'lláh does not need any of us. We must take up, day by day, month by month, the task before us. Detachment makes better instruments for Him than ambition ...[90]

Helen was at a crossroads—she longed to pioneer, yet her heart and marriage demanded another path.

What lay ahead for her in the New World was yet to be revealed.

A New Chapter: Teaching the Faith at Home

Though pioneering abroad was on hold, Helen found no shortage of opportunities to serve the Faith within North America. After years of intense activity in Europe's crowded cities, the quiet countryside of Geyserville, with its towering redwoods and the calming presence of the Russian River, provided much-needed rest. Her health had always been fragile—childhood bouts of malaria and yellow jaundice had left her vulnerable, and bronchitis was a persistent ailment. In college, she had been excused from physical activities due to recurring body aches. Now, new health concerns arose: chest swelling, an enlarged spleen, and an imbalance of red and white blood cells.

Fortunately, Geyserville's proximity to San Francisco allowed Helen to seek treatment at the University of California Hospital, where she was under the care of an excellent Italian physician, Dr Salvatore Pablo Lucia. Under his guidance, she gradually regained her strength. As her health improved, invitations from Bahá'í communities across the United States and Canada flooded in, urging the Bishops to visit and assist with teaching and deepening efforts. Expansion and consolidation were central to the Seven Year Plan, and in a vast country like the United States, the need for travel teachers was urgent.

A New Approach to Teaching

The Faith in America had undergone a significant transition since Helen's early years as a Bahá'í. As Mrs Maxwell observed:

... within recent years, the Bahá'í Cause in America was taught and spread from essentially a religious standpoint that the public were unable to bridge over to the social and moral problems of mankind, therefore its sphere of attraction was limited to those who were religiously inclined and it is only within recent years ... that we have made a new approach.[91]

This new approach aimed to make the Faith more intellectually engaging and accessible to a broader audience. Helen was particularly well-suited for this shift. With her keen intellect, excellent education, and eloquent delivery, she was a commanding presence on any stage. She carried herself with grace and radiated a deep spirituality. Horace Holley once wrote to her, remarking:

... what a privilege to meet a spiritual consciousness and not merely a personality.[92]

Helen's effectiveness as a speaker lay in her ability to connect with both the heart and the mind. In a letter to her physician, Dr Lucia, she reflected on the perception that she and Marion Holley were considered "intellectuals" among religious circles:

Among 'religious people,' Marion [Holley] and I are 'excluded' as intellectuals! This amuses us no end, for revealed to each other, we concede that the mind is not central to either of us (not that we would park it! We want to find our way around the three dimensional world) ... To be sure, we can't help wondering just how much longer intellect can be upheld as the ultimate category for this Day. To us it appears obvious that if intellect could save the race, Europe would not be fighting out its history of hatred.[93]

Honor Kempton summarised Helen's brilliance succinctly:

Your work as a teacher of the Cause ... is unique and unrivaled ... There is no one your equal—man or woman.[94]

A Life on the Road

Though Charles was not inclined toward pioneering, he could never sit still. Neither he nor Helen needed regular employment, allowing them to devote their time fully to promoting and teaching the Faith. Their dedication was evident in the miles they covered—Helen once noted that between 24 May and 1 September 1939, their car's odometer recorded over 8,000 miles of travel.

For the record, Helen never learned to drive—a task Charles took on gladly. Their constant movement made it difficult for friends to track them down. As Shirley Warde humorously remarked in a letter to Helen:

I cannot seem to find one who knows just where you are but various rumors have put you in the east, the north, and all over the map.[95]

Despite the lack of a permanent address, their mission was clear: to carry the Message of Bahá'u'lláh to every corner of the continent.

North to Alaska

After Helen's recuperation in the spring of 1938, she and Charles attended the Regional Teaching Conference in Los Angeles. There, the Guardian's passionate appeal for nine Bahá'ís to arise and settle in territories where no believer had yet resided was read and discussed. Helen's heart urged her to respond immediately, but her conscience signalled caution. That night, she had a vivid dream, which she later described in a letter to Mark Tobey:

> *On the upper story, I went from room to room, uneasy and even discontent, because I was unable to decide in which room I should work, and where I could sleep. Then the house swindled into nothingness before my gaze. It became the ether, as it were; and in the space it had occupied was a gigantic maple-leaf. The three parts were divided to make the nine points; and its color was deep and true green. The remarkable thing, however, was the upright, immovable stem; whereas the leaf moved and bowed in the breeze. I awoke contemplating this symbol and understood that it is not for us to seek security in any residence anywhere. Our*

security is to be found in the breadth of the Spirit. The divine wind will blow us where it will.[96]

One of the nine souls who immediately answered the Guardian's call was Honor Kempton, secretary of the Regional Bahá'í Teaching Committee for Arizona, California, and Nevada. A devoted and selfless Bahá'í, she had migrated to the United States from England in the early 1930s and later became an American citizen. Having lost her fiancé in World War I, she resolved never to marry and instead dedicated her life to the service of the Faith. Now, at the Los Angeles conference, she made her pledge: she would go to Alaska, a vast and spiritually untouched land that had yet to welcome a Bahá'í presence.

Following the conference, Honor wrote to Shoghi Effendi on 18 February 1939, informing him of her decision. His response, through his secretary, was immediate and filled with deep gratitude:

... he was inexpressibly delighted to know that you have spontaneously offered your services for pioneer teaching in Alaska. He can well imagine the feeling of immeasurable satisfaction and unbounded gratitude with which both the N.S.A. and the National Teaching Committee must have welcomed your determination to teach and establish the Faith in this far-off and hereto unexplored territory ... The spirit of heroic self-sacrifice, and of unflinching resolve that has prompted so noble and sacred mission ... cannot but fill all hearts with admiration and praise, and evoke the memory of those acts of unrivaled heroism, of self-less and

unstilted devotion that have characterized the lives of those immortal heroes of the Apostolic Age.[97]

Then, in his own handwriting, the Guardian added:

How proud I feel of the spirit that so powerfully animates you ... The Concourse on high acclaims your resolve and will richly bless your endeavours. Be happy and confident. Your true brother, Shoghi.[98]

A Journey Through the Redwoods

Helen and Charles offered to drive Honor to Seattle, from where she would continue her journey by boat to Anchorage. The road trip from Southern California to the Pacific Northwest was an adventure they all eagerly anticipated.

Honor wrote excitedly:

I am so tremendously excited at the thought of traveling up North and visiting all those lovely Bahá'ís ... Again, I have never seen the Redwood Highway ... It is wonderful of you and Charles to take me and it will make me feel so much happier if you are both seeing me off ... Have you read the Guardian's latest letter: **The Advent of Divine Justice?** *Marion [Holley] and I have had some wondrous moments going over it and reading it aloud. I do so wish that you were with us because your interpretation would have been invaluable. There are some inspiring passages* *and some tragic ones. It makes my heart ache to read Shoghi Effendi's appeal—and I am so glad that I have made my decision—I could not rest any longer reading such an eloquent message ...* [99]

Their two-week journey through California, Oregon, and Washington was filled with Bahá'í activities, public talks, and meetings with friends of the Faith. Finally, on 15 April 1939, the time came for Honor to embark on her mission. Helen, Charles, and several other Bahá'ís accompanied her to the pier in Seattle to see her off. By 21 April, she had arrived in Anchorage—the first Bahá'í to settle in Alaska.

A Pioneering Spirit in Alaska

For those who visit Anchorage today, it is difficult to imagine the frontier town it was in 1939—a remote settlement of just 3,000 residents, where bars outnumbered churches. The majority of its citizens were Catholic, and the Christian Science Church had a mere sixty members. Mail arrived once a week, and the local library was open only twice a week. It was an unlikely home for a cultured, educated, and refined woman like Honor Kempton, yet she had chosen this rugged outpost as her base for teaching the Faith.

She rented a small house, using one half as her residence and converting the other into 'The Book Cache—Honor Kempton's Lending Library.' This small library served as both a community hub and a means of meeting people interested in spiritual discussions. The editor of The Alaskan, a struggling newspaper, was delighted when

Honor offered to write book reviews, giving her yet another avenue to introduce Bahá'í ideas into the local culture.

Before she left for Alaska, Shoghi Effendi had written her a final word of encouragement:

> *Persevere no matter how great the obstacles in your way. Future generations will glorify your deed and emulate your example.*[100]

There would indeed be many obstacles, and not all were physical. Less than six months after she settled in Anchorage, World War II erupted in Europe. As Britain endured the Blitz, Honor's mother, brother, and sister remained in London, living through its horrors. Though far away, she carried the weight of their suffering. In a letter to Helen, she confided:

> *I feel so anxious about my dear ones in England; I feel so strongly that England will be overcome by the Nazis—at least temporarily. Sometimes I waken in the night and feel as if I had been struck—then think of England and what is coming. Oh, I know one is not supposed to think too much about things—and we know that ultimately the New World Order will come, but it is just grief over something beautiful and strong that is passing ...* [101]

Yet, despite her deep personal anguish, Honor remained steadfast. She reminded herself that she had pledged her life to Bahá'u'lláh and to Alaska:

... it is thrilling beyond words to tell of such tremendous power in the world working for good and that ultimately God's way will be our way.[102]

It was Honor Kempton's devotion to Bahá'u'lláh, her steadfastness, and her sacrifices that opened Alaska to His Cause. Less than forty years after she set foot on its shores, the Alaskan Bahá'í community elected its own National Spiritual Assembly!

Life on the Road

The pace of the Bishops' travels in 1939 was relentless, but the joy of teaching the Faith and meeting Bahá'í friends sustained them. They began the year by visiting Bahá'ís in San Diego, Pasadena, and Los Angeles, where they attended a National Spiritual Assembly session and participated in the Regional Teaching Conference. From there, they travelled north with Honor Kempton to Washington State, where she would depart for her historic pioneering journey to Alaska.

That summer, they attended the Green Acre Bahá'í School in Maine. Helen, writing to Mark Tobey, who was still in England, described their ceaseless movement:

> *Reunion with the friends is also renewal; besides, there has been an opportunity to work, stimulated, as we are by the demands ... The N.S.A. is in session. On Monday we will trail Roy [Wilhelm] to the camp of goats. Next week, Boston, then New York. We will visit Mrs. Movius in Buffalo and help with the teaching work; the Collinsons in Geneva; Louhelen afterward ... Now the Siegfrieds have invited us to Montreal ...* [103]

Between September 1937 (when they returned to the United States) and September 1939, the Bishops had attended nearly every Bahá'í summer school in North America. Among them, Green Acre held a special place in Helen's heart. She confided to Mrs Maxwell, in her characteristic directness:

> *I have never been in an environment of Bahá'í community where the work was not regimented for most of the hours, leaving but little time for the solitude we need for meditation and reading... In this respect, the English summer school, of which we enjoyed two sessions, was not strenuous; yet sociability took the place of quietude. The German sessions were a bit long for my concentration. And Geyserville has racehorse speed, rushed as it is into a fortnight a month's session ... You can imagine with your insight, May, how much delight I have had in three weeks at Green Acre.* [104]

But while the Bishops were travel-teaching and helping to lay the foundation of a new world order in the old world, war was on the horizon. The post-World War I days of fragile peace were about to end. The communist threat in Germany, among many other causes, helped bring Hitler and his Nazi Party to power in 1933, and from then on, the dictator began his plan of redrawing the map of Europe. He annexed Austria, divided and then took Czechoslovakia, and finally woke up the French and the British when his army crossed the Polish border on 1 September 1939. Europe's Civil War that had begun in 1914, followed by a fragile truce in 1918, erupted once more.

On that September day, the Bishops, at home in Geyserville, did not hear the news on the air since they did not have a radio, but as was their custom, they walked to the village in the morning and purchased the daily newspaper, and the headline told the grim story.

The British Bahá'í Community and the War

When the war began in Europe, most Americans believed that it was Europe's problem alone and that the ultimate triumph of Britain and France over Germany was assured since they had between them the world's two greatest empires, the world's greatest navy and army, and control of almost unlimited material resources. Gallup polls indicated that most Americans believed that what was happening in Europe was not, and should not be their concern. Americans were still struggling with their own economic problems and resolving them was by far their top priority.

Meanwhile, the Congress of the United States in October 1939—on the recommendation of President Roosevelt—amended America's Neutrality Act with a 'cash and carry provision' by which Americans were allowed to sell arms and war supplies to other nations as long as recipients paid cash for what they purchased and transported their supplies on their own ships. As intended, this amendment primarily benefited the two Allied powers, as they had both the money and the ships to take advantage of it. The billions of dollars that France and Great Britain spent in the United States for their military and non-military needs proved to be the catalyst for America's economic recovery from the Great Depression.

By the summer of 1940, Germany had occupied most of what was Poland (and what was left of that country, Hitler presented to Stalin) and its armed forces had overwhelmed the French and the British armies on the Western Front, occupying Holland, Belgium, Norway, and Luxembourg in the process. Hitler was, by then, practically master of the whole continent. Mussolini was his ally, and Hitler enjoyed a treaty of non-aggression with Stalin. Only Great Britain remained defiant.

Faith and Conflict

For Helen, who had only recently returned from Europe after serving the Faith for three years and forming deep friendships, the war was not a distant concern. To her, England was a second home; she loved and respected its Bahá'í community and treasured the memory of such outstanding followers of Bahá'u'lláh as George Townshend, David Hofman, Hasan Balyuzi, John and Dorothy

Ferraby, and many others. She found some relief in the knowledge that Lady Blomfield, in whose home she had so often spoken about the New World Order, had passed to the Abha Kingdom

> *serenely and before the terrible blitz. For the very thought that humanity was plunged into another war was more than she could endure after having taken such a notable part in the spiritual planning of peace.*[105]

From the outset, Helen shared deeply in the hardships of her British friends. However, all that she and many other American Bahá'ís could do at the time was send packages of food, clothing, and other essentials to those suffering under war conditions.

As the Battle of Britain raged, there were only seven Bahá'í National Spiritual Assemblies in the world: Iran, the United States/Canada, Egypt, Iraq, India/Burma, Australia/New Zealand, and Great Britain. The report of the National Spiritual Assembly of Great Britain for The Bahá'í World: 1940-44 is succinct yet telling:

> *The history of the British Bahá'í community in the years 1940-44 is a history of wartime, of new and scarcely anticipated circumstances, of difficulties, of depleted communities, but yet, in spite of all this, a record of slow and not yet entirely visible, but nevertheless, very definite progress.*[106]

The Guardian instructed the National Assembly of Great Britain that Bahá'ís should seek non-combatant assignments, and the Assembly printed a statement outlining the Bahá'í position on military service to assist both individuals and authorities making inquiries. Among British Bahá'ís, only one, Robert Yool, served in a fighting unit. Having been a reservist before becoming a Bahá'í, he continued in service and was awarded the Distinguished Conduct Medal for bravery during the North African campaign, where he saved a comrade from a burning tank.

Wartime Challenges and Adaptations

The British Bahá'í summer school in 1940 was cancelled due to the threat of a German invasion, and the following year, no location could be secured to host one. Instead, at the Bahá'í Centre in the industrial town of Bradford, weekend study classes were organised. In 1942, two long-weekend study sessions were held—one in Torquay, in the south, and the other in Buxton, in the north.

A British Bahá'í from Torquay, Lilian Stevens, described the difficult circumstances in a letter to Helen:

> *So much has happened in the last few months that I scarcely know where to begin. You know that we had established a Center here and were making slow but sure progress. In June, the government took over the whole building, so we have now a room somewhere else for one afternoon a week.*[107]

She added that what was happening in Torquay was typical of all Bahá'í communities in Great Britain, yet

> *… everyone here is very calm, and very determined to help in every way possible, and if there is nothing we can do — well,*

to keep cheerful and not to get in the way of those who are doing important work.[108]

By 1943, the situation had improved to the point where Bahá'ís were able to hold a summer school in a lovely house in the heart of Warwickshire. Despite their small numbers, Bahá'ís managed to hold celebrations in London, Torquay, and Manchester for the Centenary of the Declaration of the Báb in 1944. Helen, eager to contribute to the occasion, sent ingredients for a celebratory cake via the Ferraby family, for which she received a gracious letter of thanks from Mrs Ferraby.

By then, the British National Spiritual Assembly had launched a Six-Year Plan to be completed by 1950—the Centenary of the Báb's Martyrdom—focusing on the establishment of nineteen local assemblies spread across different parts of the British Isles.

Reflections on Britain's Future

During the height of the Battle of Britain, Honor Kempton, writing from her pioneering post in Alaska on 1 June 1940, asked Helen whether the Guardian had made any remarks about the fate of Great Britain after the war during their pilgrimage in 1934. Helen replied that no specific predictions were given, but she reiterated what she had already shared—that England stood to lose its colonies. Understanding Honor's deep concern for her homeland, Helen sought to offer perspective:

You know that I am Anglophile and that I grieve to think of the chaos for the period when, after a weakened British Common Law—without doubt the highest achievement of Christian civilization—the renegade nations and aggressors with their uncurbed appetites begin to resist the Divine Law revealed by the Manifestation unto the nations. You know the passage where the Master says, 'ere long the hosts of India and China, Africa, etc. will arise to resist His Cause. Then will the knights of the Covenant assisted by hosts from on high arise to make manifest the truth of the saying, 'Behold what confusion hath overtaken the infidels.' (Please do not give that out because it is not exact. First verify the words—the meaning is right, I am certain ...) Where ever there is British Common Law there are human rights that can not be disputed ... The Master told Lord Lamington at the time of the Armistice of '18: 'the present is dark. The immediate future is darker still. The distant future is immeasurably bright.' And, again and again, He referred to the mighty works of the spirit that would come from the British people after the cycle of their historical empire was completed.[109]

The Publishing of The Promised Day Is Come

It is most remarkable that in 1941, during the darkest hours of the Battle of Britain, the beloved Guardian wrote a lengthy letter addressed to the Bahá'ís of the West, titled *The Promised Day Is Come*, which begins:

A tempest, unprecedented in its violence, unpredictable in its course, catastrophic in its immediate effects, unimaginably glorious in its ultimate consequence, is sweeping the face of the earth. Humanity gripped in the clutches of its devastating power, is smitten by the evidences of its resistless fury. It can neither perceive its origin, nor probe its significance, nor discern its outcome. Bewildered, agonized, and helpless, it watches this great and mighty wind of God, invading the remotest and fairest regions of the earth, rocking its foundations, deranging its equilibrium, sundering its nations, disrupting the home of its peoples, wasting its cities, driving into exile its kings, pulling down its bulwarks, uprooting its institutions, dimming its light, and harrowing up the souls of its inhabitants.[110]

In this message, Shoghi Effendi quoted extensively from the Tablets and letters of Bahá'u'lláh addressed to the rulers of the earth—monarchs such as Napoleon III, Queen Victoria, Tsar Alexander II, Wilhelm of Prussia, Franz Joseph I of the Austro-Hungarian Empire, the Sultan of Turkey, and Nasiri'd-Din Shah of Iran, as well as the ecclesiastical leaders of Christianity and Islam. These warnings, the Guardian explained, were the roadmap for human salvation, but the rulers and religious leaders had ignored the Message, thereby forfeiting their legitimacy. Humanity was suffering the consequences of its leaders' vanity and rejection of divine guidance.

However, *The Promised Day Is Come* was not simply a pronouncement of humanity's failures. It, as Horace Holley later observed:

... restored the integrity of religion in human experience, and disclosed the unique and universal character of the Dispensation of Bahá'u'lláh. In this volume the world has light for darkness, healing for its hurt, guidance for its future, justice for its wrongs, purification for its evils. [111]

While reflecting on the chaotic and tragic human condition, Shoghi Effendi was not condemning human nature but rather affirming that light would ultimately follow darkness. He reminded the world that Bahá'u'lláh's Revelation had come to

... forge with the hammer of His Will, and through the fire of tribulation, upon the anvil of this travailing age ... these scattered and mutually destructive fragments into which a perverse world has fallen, into one single unit, solid, and indivisible, able to execute His design for the children of men. [112]

The Guardian's message concluded with an uplifting assurance:

Ours rather the duty, however confused the scene, however dismal the present outlook, however circumscribed the resources we dispose of, to labor serenely, confidently and unremittingly to lend our share of assistance, in whichever way circumstances may enable us, to the operation of forces which, as marshaled and directed by Bahá'u'lláh, are leading humanity out of the valley of misery and shame to the loftiest summit of power and glory. [113]

The Bahá'í Response in the Midst of War

To Bahá'ís everywhere, but particularly in the West, *The Promised Day Is Come* was a further confirmation that, amidst the destruction of the old order, their mandate remained unchanged: to build the foundations of a new world order.

From 1 September 1939 to 7 December 1941, Americans were not officially engaged in the war, but unofficially, they were very much a part of it. A year after passing the Neutrality Act of 1939, Franklin Roosevelt provided, practically as a gift, 50 'old' American destroyers to the British Navy for their home defence.

In 1941, the US Congress went further by passing the Lend-Lease Act, effectively providing an unlimited line of credit to the Allies. This act allowed any nation deemed vital to American security to lease war materials from the United States, paying for what was used or lost and returning what remained after the war. In essence, the Lend-Lease Act was America's economic declaration of war on the Axis Powers, immediately supplying the British Commonwealth with billions of dollars in military and non-military aid.

The Seven Year Plan : Latin America

From the beginning, one of the most ambitious goals of the Seven Year Plan was the establishment of at least one spiritual assembly in every Latin American republic. In 1939, the National Spiritual Assembly formed the Inter-America Committee, appointing Loulie Matthews as its chairperson and Sara Kenny as secretary. Among its members were Helen Bishop, Amelia Collins, Leroy Ioas, Myrtle Dodge, and ER Matthews. Additional associate members included Mrs AE Stewart, Siegfried Schopflocher, and Pedro Espinosa of Mexico City.

The Matthews generously donated their 20-acre estate in Colorado Springs to train those preparing for pioneering or travel teaching in Latin America. Helen, in collaboration with Loulie, selected passages from the writings of Bahá'u'lláh and 'Abdu'l-Bahá, translating them into Spanish to provide new believers with a representative collection of sacred texts.

In 1940, Helen was appointed committee secretary, and that year, forty-nine pioneers were trained at the institute. However, the committee faced a serious challenge south of the border. In Mexico City, a young Bahá'í community had become deeply divided due to the influence of Ahmad Sohrab's *New History Society*. The Guardian urged the North American Bahá'í community to send experienced teachers to reconcile the community. Not surprisingly, the National Spiritual Assembly called upon the Bishops, and in the winter of 1940, Charles and Helen travelled to Mexico—a place that held deep personal meaning for Helen, as it was her birthplace.

Upon arrival in the capital, they found a fractured Bahá'í community. The Covenant-Breakers had created significant discord. Prior to their arrival, Juliet Thompson, Mrs Smythe, and Helen Campbell of New York had made repeated attempts to restore unity, but with little success. Helen believed that 'Juliet's intensive "love" was not a healing for this situation,' but neither was Helen's method that 'was quietly, subtly, yet categorically rejected by [a local Bahá'í] with the statement that "my American method" would not be useful to them and that he would continue his series of lectures.' 'By invitation,' Helen wrote to Honor Kempton, 'we attended four meetings. After that, we were invited no longer. No hard words on either side.' [114]

Despite this resistance, the Bishops' time in Mexico was not without its successes. Helen gave several well-attended lectures in Spanish, receiving positive press coverage. In Mazatlán, a public lecture drew a large audience, and she later sent a list of promising contacts to the National Teaching Committee. In Sinaloa, she was invited to speak at a Masonic gathering, where an audience of over one hundred delegates and guests engaged enthusiastically with her message. Unfortunately, US government restrictions on printed materials prevented the Bishops from carrying Bahá'í literature across international borders, but Helen later sent pamphlets to those she had met.

These experiences in Mexico provided a glimpse of the challenges ahead in fulfilling the Seven Year Plan's Latin American objectives.

The Seven Year Plan : Home Front

On the home front, the National Teaching Committee—chaired by Leroy Ioas and with Charlotte Linfoot as secretary—launched an ambitious public teaching campaign in late 1940. The plan aimed to bring outstanding Bahá'í speakers to major cities such as Chicago, New York, and Boston at two or three-month intervals. Local assemblies were tasked with securing publicity, radio engagements, and invitations from clubs and service organizations. Meanwhile, regional teaching committees were to organize circuit teaching within their areas.

A significant obstacle, however, was the limited number of Bahá'í speakers capable of fulfilling the plan's goals. Helen was among the few qualified individuals. On 15 August 1940, Charlotte Linfoot wrote to Helen, inquiring whether she could commit two months to teaching on the East Coast, offering financial assistance if needed. Helen regretfully declined:

> As this is the first assignment offered by the National Teaching Committee, I am sorrier than otherwise to have to say 'no'.[115]

She explained that economic constraints made such an undertaking impossible, that 'this has been a lean year for us.'

The Bishops had just returned from Mexico, and financial difficulties compelled them to carefully manage their expenses. Although the Bishop Trust had supported their work, economic reverses had severely restricted its funds, forcing the couple to 'count every penny.' Not until March 1943, with the passing of Uncle Faxon, did Charles receive a secure inheritance.

Helen further explained her refusal, that she is not

> *... willing to give up my amateur status ... that is to say, I feel it would be unethical for me to accept financial aid for teaching because I have domestic obligations which do not permit me to give even for a period my whole time to speaking and teaching.*[116]

She remained mindful of the Guardian's advice to be a devoted wife to Charles and could not justify leaving him alone for such an extended period.

Public Speaking and the Challenge of Restrictions

In September 1940, the National Teaching Committee invited Helen to address 800–1,000 teachers at a conference in Coeur d'Alene, Idaho. However, the event's theme—public education—prohibited any direct mention of religion. Helen's response was firm:

> *Bahá'u'lláh's Message is the only message worth hearing ... [it's proclamation is] the only worthwhile expenditure of time, money and energy ... Not having a surplus of any of these three, I have learned to be tough and say 'no'.*[117]

A few months later, Robert Gulick at Chico State College in California, succeeded in arranging for Helen to address the entire student body. When he happily informed Helen of the date, she was delighted to accept, thinking, naturally, that she was to talk about the Faith. However, her assumption proved to be wrong, because not long before her invitation, Marzieh Gail had spoken at the same college before students of history, geography, and international relations on the basic Bahá'í principles relating to those subjects. Even though her presentations had been well received, leading to placement of Bahá'í books in the college library, her talks had caused college administrators to think again about the legality of religious presentations at a state-supported college such as theirs.

The president of the college then reminded Robert Gulick of the sensitive line that had to be drawn in academia and insisted that there be no direct mention of the Faith. But the date for the lecture had been set, the lecturer approved, and publicity given to college media, though no mention of the title of the lecture! To save the day, the president suggested 'Use of Freedom' as a safe topic.

Robert reluctantly had to inform Helen of the arrangement. Her reaction was predictable. How could she talk on 'freedom' where in fact there was none!

'It is my rule not to accepting invitations to speak in parochial schools or even clubs, where religious propaganda is taboo,' she wrote to Robert. She elaborated:

> *The inhibition is so painful to me that it makes my speaking an ordeal. Bahá'í is so thoroughly interwoven with my fabric of consciousness that I cannot well sustain a half-hour's discourse without building the Cause into it—not using*

> *the name Bahá'u'lláh or 'Abdu'l-Bahá does not alter that persistent borrowing.*
>
> *More than a psychological handicap, the premise was ethically wrong. If there is a law against instructing religious propaganda in state schools, we ought not to break it. The Guardian made it clear on several occasions; the dignity of the Cause requires that we do not infringe upon the rules of societies or the laws of the state. It is not for us to usurp privileges or curry favors for God.*[118]

However, Helen conceded that it was too late to cancel the talk, and she informed Robert that her plan is to speak on the essence of freedom:

> *… that is search for the truth and then present the audience with the Bahá'í plan for a world commonwealth.*[119]

But at the last-minute, the school administration, still uneasy about the subject of the lecture, decided to change it to 'Latin America' without informing the lecturer!

The drive from San Francisco to Chico on a beautiful spring day was pleasant, and upon arrival, Helen and Charles were welcomed by Alice Anderson and her father, 'two Bahá'ís that we had met and recognized in many countries—the world-workers.'

Helen was accompanied by the president of the college to the lecture hall 'to make sure that I would not step outside of the legal boundary.' After her lecture on Latin America, the president thanked her and commented: 'That, Mrs. Bishop, was an utterly delightful talk.' The compliment was graciously received, but what was much more rewarding to Helen was the simple comment of a young man who approached her and said 'thanks.' Helen asked him, 'Why?' The student said that 'it was not an ordinary lecture; behind [your] words there was a compelling power that was from spirit.' Those simple words, Helen thought, affirmed 'how much the Name is needed where we can use it.'[120]

Upon returning home, she received a letter from Alice Anderson, who acknowledged Helen's struggle in balancing the limitations imposed on her speech with her unwavering commitment to the Cause:

> *Warm-heartedly Marzieh [Gail] wrote me in this wise: 'Talks of that sort are never easy for me to give, because I feel—here is all this bread that has come down from heaven, and all we can share with people is crumbs...'*[121]

The Passing of Mrs May Maxwell

On 23 April 1940, Bahá'í pioneers across Latin America—some alone, others in the company of newly formed believers—joined North American Bahá'ís in commemorating the ascension of one of the Faith's most revered heroines, Mrs May Maxwell, to the Abhá Kingdom. In his tribute, the Guardian honoured her station:

> Laden with the fruits garnered through well-nigh half a century of toilsome service to the Cause she so greatly loved, and afire with the longing to worthily demonstrate her gratitude in her overwhelming awareness of the bounties of her Lord and Master, she set her face toward the southern outposts of the Faith in the New World, and laid down her life in such a spirit of consecration and self-sacrifice as has truly merited the crown of martyrdom.[122]

Shoghi Effendi, in a cablegram to May's husband, William Sutherland Maxwell, expressed his condolences and paid tribute to her life of service:

> Her tomb, designed by yourself, erected by me, on the spot where she fought, and fell gloriously, will become a historic center of pioneer Bahá'í activity.[123]

Earlier that year, Mrs Maxwell and her niece, Jeanne Bolles, had pioneered to Argentina, intending to help establish an assembly in Buenos Aires. In a deeply personal letter from Haifa, Rúḥíyyih Khánum shared a remarkable insight with Dr Ali Kuli Khan:

> Now I will tell you something that is very strange which I have never told anyone. One day, over a year ago, when I was sitting with our beloved Guardian, and he had been reading reports of the work in South America—he suddenly said to me, 'You know what your Mother should do? She should

go to South America and die there serving the Cause—that is what she should do!' I admit that I was alarmed at such words! I said 'how could I live if I were never to see her again?' And the thought terrified me and I said 'Do you want me to tell her this?' But he said No, it was not necessary! and I felt greatly relieved! It shows that I was not very heroic—I just could not send her! But I never forgot it. And so when Mother mentioned, en passant, that she felt a longing to go and teach there after talking to Mrs. Stewart. (Mrs. Frances Benedict Stewart had gone pioneering in Argentina in 1936 and again in 1939 and by her effort a Bahá'í Group had been established there) I went at once to the Guardian and asked him if I could cable her that he approved of her desire. He said yes and so I did. If I had not pushed her [to] open the door by sending the encouragement of the Guardian, I doubt if she could have overcome the obstacle of my father's alarm at such a thought [given] her own wariness physically, her run-down condition. So praise be to God in the end I did not hold her back, although it was a terrible feeling to know she had gone so much further away from me![124]

A Profound Loss

Marion Holley, reflecting on May Maxwell's passing, wrote to Helen:

There is so much I want to say to you that comes to my mind, as I have pondered over you and me and May and Keith (Ransom-Kehler). For are we not, both children of these unique spirits, but in different proportions? You had the spiritual qualities by nature; you had them from earliest childhood. To these May appealed and doubtless gave them an additional fire. But Keith came in six years to fructify your mind. But I was another creature, all intellect (of a sort), all logic and critical, analytical power without much effort[,] the superficial rationality of our West Coast Bahá'ís. No one but Keith could have conquered this quality in me, not because I had an exceptionally good mind, but because I was stubborn. To this day, I might not [have not been won over to] the Cause, had she not come to our home. So she won me upon my own ground. But May evoked the dormant life—the spirit of faith and love which had had no outward expression. It is because of May that you say I am a Persian! And it is this spirit that I need always—the increase of it to unguessed depth—for the mode of my life and the native bent of my individuality will always keep me practical, efficient, able to cope with a material world. And you, dearest one, need this too—the ardor which was Keith's in such poignant measure.[125]

The news of May Maxwell's passing was deeply distressing to Helen. From the beginning of her Bahá'í journey, she had known, loved, respected, and admired May. In a letter to William Sutherland Maxwell, Helen conveyed her grief and gratitude:

Although I share, as a member of the Inter-American Committee in the telegram of sympathy in your bereavement (and I was with Charles, by Mrs Mathews' side when she sent it from Palm Springs) yet I long to follow that collective expression of grief with my own testimony of gratitude and remembrance to May. All those among the friends throughout the world who have experienced May's love and inspiration cannot forget her. First and foremost in that company will be Rúḥíyyih Khánum, who, in her own destiny, is the continuation of May's being in this world. A blessed family you are ... [126]

Preserving a Legacy

Helen strongly believed that a biography of May Maxwell should be written and suggested to William Sutherland Maxwell that Marion Holley be the one to undertake the task:

... for the love she had for May—and the love May bore her will find its instrument in a great literary talent. How beautiful that the Guardian reached out to give her the pen! assuredly, Marion will be confirmed by that Power without which all effort is uncreative. [127]

Helen sent Marion all the letters she had received from May since their first correspondence in 1926. In response, Marion acknowledged the great value of these letters, remarking that they had 'filled many gaps in my dates and my knowledge of her psychology during [those many] years.' [128]

Chapter 4

AMERICA AT WAR

Chapter 4

Purified in the Crucible of a Common War

America officially entered the Second World War on 8 December 1941, a day after the Japanese air attack on Pearl Harbor. For months, the government of General Hideki Tojo, confident of its alliance with Germany and Italy—but without consulting these allies—had secretly prepared for war against the United States. On 7 December, Japanese naval and air forces struck Pearl Harbor, and within two hours, Americans had lost eight battleships, three cruisers, three destroyers, almost 200 airplanes, and more than 2,400 military personnel and civilians. Life in the United States changed dramatically on that day, and so did the course of human history.

When the Bishops heard that war had been declared against Japan, both recalled that back in 1933 while in the Holy Land, the Guardian warned them that the Pacific would be the storm centre of the fiercest fighting and commented that Americans should erase the Atlantic and Pacific oceans from their world-view, only then they would have a realistic picture of their country's strategic position.[129] Helen also reminded her husband of the Guardian's prophetic statement in *The Advent of Divine Justice*:

The immediate future must, as a result of this steady, this gradual, and inevitable absorption in the manifold perplexities and problems afflicting humanity, be dark and oppressive for that nation. The world-shaking ordeal which Bahá'u'lláh, as quoted in the foregoing pages, has so graphically prophesied, may find it swept, to an unprecedented degree, into its vortex. Out of it will probably emerge, unlike its reactions to the last world conflict, consciously determined to seize its opportunity, to bring the full weight of its influence to bear upon the gigantic problems that such an ordeal must leave in its wake, and to exorcise forever, in conjunction with its sister nations of both the East and the West, the greatest curse which, from time immemorial, has afflicted and degraded the human race. Then, and only then, will the American nation, molded and purified in the crucible of a common war, inured to its rigors, and disciplined by its lessons, be in a position to raise its voice in the councils of the nations, itself lay the cornerstone of a universal and enduring peace, proclaim the solidarity, the unity, and maturity of mankind, and assist in the establishment of the promised reign of righteousness on earth.[130]

A New Way of Life

Like all Americans, the Bishops were immediately affected by their country's entry into the global conflict. The days when they could travel freely were over; gasoline was rationed, making their service to the Faith through travel teaching far more challenging. Since their return from Europe, they had viewed the village of Geyserville as a convenient but temporary residence, not a permanent home. Helen confided to Horace Holley, 'we are not farmers and we are not in the right place.'[131]

Charles wanted to move closer to the House of Worship in Wilmette, Illinois, but the attack on Pearl Harbor had a direct impact on his income. The federal government froze all assets in Hawaii, leaving an uncertain future for the sugar industry, on which the Bishop Trust largely depended. Japanese labour was now forbidden in the islands, further jeopardizing their financial situation. 'Mail bearing income checks' Helen wrote to Charlotte Linfoot 'are subject to censorship and unpredictable delay.'[132]

Helen, however, preferred to live in San Francisco, a city she loved and whose Bahá'í community she admired. But the financial uncertainty and the possibility of seeking employment made this option unrealistic. Given these circumstances, the Bishops decided to move to Southern California, where there were more job opportunities and several active Bahá'í communities within a reasonable distance—allowing them to continue serving without exhausting their gasoline allotment. For Helen, an added attraction was the significant Latino population to whom she could present Bahá'u'lláh's Message in Spanish.

By January 1942, the Bishops had rented a house at 476 South Euclid Avenue in Pasadena. Almost immediately, Charles was selected to the Regional Teaching Committee for California and Nevada (alongside Mr. and Mrs. William Sears and Mrs. James E. Crouchley) and was elected to Pasadena's Spiritual Assembly. By the end of the year, the

US Office of Price Administration issued a decision granting Bahá'í administrative officers preferred mileage, stating:

> *Upon the review of the facts presented by representatives of the Bahá'í Faith, we conclude that the chairmen and secretaries of the local Assemblies of the Bahá'ís may be eligible for preferred mileage under the provision of section 7706 (K) to meet the religious needs of the localities they regularly serve.* [133]

This meant Charles could now obtain a 'B' ration card for gasoline, allowing for greater travel opportunities.

Fortunately, the Bishops did not have to compromise their financial independence, as restrictions on Hawaiian fund transfers were lifted. Additionally, 'Uncle Faxon' soon passed away, leaving Charles a trust fund share that provided financial security. Helen explained the terms of the will to her brother Robert:

> *No capital, you know, but a Trust Fund in which he [Charles] shares the income with his sister and brothers ... [the income is now enough] to enable us to change the style of living we have held to these past seven years.* [134]

New Responsibilities

In Pasadena, Charles and Helen embraced a more settled lifestyle for the first time in their married life. They cultivated a victory garden and even took up bread baking. Charles became a Warden in Civil Defence, while Helen served as a neighbourhood Day Warden.

As the United States entered the war, the National Spiritual Assembly, through Bahá'í News, relayed the Guardian's instructions regarding military service. Bahá'ís were encouraged to participate in civil defence and humanitarian efforts as individuals, while the community and its institutions were to 'confine their efforts to direct Bahá'í work and discharge of the functions definitely assigned them in teaching.'

In 1942, the National Spiritual Assembly created a College Speakers Bureau to expand presentations about the Faith beyond race relations to encompass broader Bahá'í themes. Two distinguished Bahá'ís, Louis Gregory and Dorothy Baker, had already set high standards through their college presentations. That year, Dorothy Baker spoke at more than 100 colleges and universities, primarily in the South and Southwest, while Louis Gregory addressed over fifty college audiences, mostly at historically Black institutions. Their presentations were met with enthusiastic responses.

President R. B. Atwood of Kentucky State College wrote to Horace Holley:

In the thirteen years of my administrative experience as the chief executive of this college, no speaker has appeared upon our platform with a message more comprehensive in nature, more universal in scope and more gripping in its appeal. For some forty minutes, Mrs. Baker gained and held the complete attention of our audience. While some of us had been introduced to the Bahá'í Movement in other institutions, so far as I know, Mrs. Baker is the first to bring the message to Kentucky State College. We are grateful to you for sending her and to her coming.[135]

Similarly, President JL Hartman of Bowling Green Business University commented:

We are accustomed of having extraordinary speakers, but I cannot recall that we ever listened to a woman who so pleased everybody as Mrs. Baker. Her personality, the orderliness of her address, her general grooming were extraordinary; but the best part of her address was the high ideals she held ... Every school in America ought to hear Mrs. Baker. She spreads the gospel of everlasting truth ... We are grateful to your organization, or to some body, for her appearance here.[136]

The National Spiritual Assembly invited Helen to join the College Speakers Bureau, but war-related travel restrictions and the prolonged separation from Charles made participation difficult. She respectfully declined.

Meanwhile, the war years in California became a golden era for Bahá'í firesides. Regular and well-attended meetings were held throughout the Bay Area and Southern California. The Bishops hosted a weekly fireside at their home, and Helen was often a guest speaker at other locations. These gatherings attracted an increasing number of individuals, including members of the entertainment industry. Helen recorded in her journal that on one evening in 1942, character actor OZ Whitehead 'declared his Faith in Bahá'u'lláh' at her home.

A Visit with Shoghi Effendi's Oxford Tutor

In December 1943, Sir Alexander Lindsay, the Master of Balliol College, visited California at the invitation of the Athenaeum—an affiliate of 'the patrons and patronesses of [the] California Technical Institute'—to deliver a lecture entitled 'Freedom.' At a time when the world was engulfed in war, the subject was timely. Mr and Mrs Stuart French, a Bahá'í couple and close friends of the Bishops, were members of the Athenaeum and offered their lecture invitations to the Bishops. Helen and Charles were eager to attend, not just for the message, but because the speaker had been Shoghi Effendi's tutor at Oxford University two decades earlier.

Sir Alexander's lecture was as impressive as expected. As soon as it ended, well-wishers and admirers surrounded him. Helen longed for an opportunity to speak with him but, as she later expressed in her report to Shoghi Effendi, 'not as a Los Angeles crackpot who must bring up his vegetarianism or psychism or other mania on every occasion. I felt that I must begin where he was—not with my thoughts for the Faith and my heart with the Guardian.'[137]

However, with so many gathered around him, she struggled to find a private moment. Charles, sensing the difficulty, advised her to give up and leave for home. They walked to the car, and Charles started driving. But as Helen later described:

> *We were half a short distance between the College and our cottage when I saw with the speed of a flash of lightning the whole theme of his discourse in relation to the world of Divine Revelation. He had placed this bold emphasis (not upon economics as the popular 'isms' do in the universities)—not even politics, which is understandable in our present crisis—but upon freedom of speech as the element of democratic institutions. He had held the right to petition ... the first index of the survival of free institutions today: he held that with the right of the common man to make his needs and hardships known, all problems of economics and politics can be solved because free discussion and consultation inform all members of the society of the common danger and therefore has 'survival value.' But he did not say why the word among men is important and why it must be preserved against all absolutists.*[138]

Helen pleaded with Charles to return to the campus; and her good-natured and patient husband did as she wished. By the time they entered the lecture hall, the crowd had shrunk, and Helen found the good professor flanked only by 'two old ladies with forty-dollar hats.' Apparently, the tall Master of Balliol College was relieved by her presence because he looked over the heads of the ladies at her and asked: 'What do you think?'[139] The ladies must have realized that their time was over and bid him good-bye.

Sir Alexander took Helen's arm and led her to the centre of the hall where a pair of Chesterfield sofas faced each other before a roaring fire. After few short and inconsequential remarks, Helen asked the professor:

> *Why is the 'Word' the civilizing medium? Is it because the speech of men is only a reflection of the speaking of God through revelation and the Prophets. He murmured something non-committal and turned from me to the fire. He looked into the fire. Then he looked into eternity ... His gravity was beautiful to behold, Shoghi Effendi, there was a pull toward him, as if ideas were flowing his way, and he was grasping them and commanding them. I saw that he had forgotten me, that he saw something I did not see, and that he was in the realm of ideas. Wherever he was it was gratifying to him.*[140]

In his response, Sir Alexander spoke of Jesus and the influence of His Words over men, but that was "about all that he acknowledged." He again emphasized that the common man was capable and could learn to understand the problems that had confronted man in past ages. He added that dictators had done all the talking and the repetition of concepts tended to replace freedom of action in the common man.

Helen found the direction of the conversation unsatisfying. Seeking common ground, she mentioned that she had represented the International Bahá'í Bureau at the 1936 World Congress of Faiths in London. Sir Alexander recalled the event but mentioned he had not been in the city at the time.

Finally, she asked what had brought her to the lecture in the first place:

> Was Shoghi Effendi at Balliol during your time?

Undisguised tenderness flooded his voice:

> Did I know him? I suffered for him—that that I did. I had posted my schedule ... and Shoghi Effendi came to me asking, 'what do you do between seven and half past eight?' 'Why man,' I cried, 'I dine!' 'Oh,' said Shoghi Effendi with obvious disappointment, 'but must you have all that time?' I had not found that much eagerness for knowledge at Oxford! So I gave him another quarter hour and went with less dinner! So it was: I suffered for Him![141]

Then the tutor, with tenderness, continued:

> Shoghi Effendi's idea of education was to discover somebody whose opinions he valued and then question him ... [142]

Helen could see he was thoroughly enjoying the recollection, performing his role as the long-suffering tutor with flair. He commented on the exceptional mind and intellect of his former pupil, and with a sense of disappointment adds:

> *Quite after that we lost him. He left us to become the head of a religion. What a pity!*

Sir Alexander was referring to the fact that the young man, before finishing his degree, had to return to Haifa to assume Guardianship of the Bahá'í Faith.

Helen, noticing the tutor's regrets, asked him whether he had read any of Shoghi Effendi's writings since he became the Guardian. Proudly he answered that his gifted student had kept in touch with him and had sent him copies of his books: 'I have them in my library.' Helen, however, felt that, alas, he had not read them, otherwise he would not have made the comment about 'his loss to the intellectual world.'

Sir Alexander, a confirmed humanist, did not believe that there was anything in religion that man could not achieve by his own efforts. Realizing that the dialogue had reached a dead end, Helen told the professor that she had concerns about his cold and thanked him for hearing her out. She writes to the beloved Guardian:

> *He searched my face in his canny style you know so well, and said quietly but not without unction, 'I thank you.'*[143]

An Encounter with Dr Jordan

Soon after that visit, Helen had an opportunity to meet another distinguished educator, though one with quite different philosophical and religious values from the Oxford professor. She read in some Los Angeles-area newspapers that a well-known American Presbyterian missionary to Iran, now back in the US, was to be the guest of one of Pasadena's most prominent churches and would deliver its Sunday sermon.

He was Samuel Martin Jordan, 'a tall, twinkling-eyed man with a cherubic face and a small, comical beard' who went to Iran as a young missionary before the country's Constitutional Revolution of 1906 and had remained there ever since.

The Rise of Missionary Activity in the Middle East

Christian missionary interest in the Middle East in the modern era can be traced back to the beginning of the 19th century when a powerful religious-revival movement, called by some historians the Second Great Awakening, was sweeping the Christian world. Many, particularly within Protestant churches, believed that the return of Christ was imminent and that His Second Coming would occur only once the entire world was 'evangelised.'

With great enthusiasm and optimism, thousands of missionaries settled in Africa, Asia, the Pacific Islands, and the Middle East to preach the Gospel, convinced that with divine assistance, the two-thirds of the world's population who were not Christian would be brought under the banner of His Kingdom within a generation.

Missionaries and the Ottoman Empire's Religious System

For the hundreds of Christian missionaries who went to the Ottoman Empire, the administration of the empire must have been an unanticipated and shocking revelation. The Turks, who had ruled over large sections of North Africa, most of the Middle East west of Iran, and even parts of Europe for more than four hundred years, practised a rigid but remarkably tolerant religious policy. They called it 'millet,' a system under which the population of the empire was divided by religion rather than geography, ethnicity, or language.

Each 'millet,' such as Greek Orthodox, Armenian Orthodox, Muslim, or Jewish, was subject to the authority of its own religious hierarchy. Adherents were free to change their religious affiliations if they wished—so a Jew could become Catholic, or a Greek Orthodox could become a Presbyterian, for example. The only exception applied to the Islamic 'millet.' Once you belonged to it, you could not change your religious identity—the penalty for doing so was death.

Given these circumstances, it is not surprising that few Turks accepted baptism from the missionaries. After about two decades of futile attempts by well-intentioned, often eloquent preachers of the Gospel, only a few dozen converted.

A Shift from Evangelisation to Education

By the middle of the 19th century, the focus of Christian missionaries in the Middle East shifted from evangelisation to education and health. By the end of the century, they had founded several modern hospitals and health clinics and established hundreds of schools, from primary schools to universities. Some of these institutions attained outstanding academic credentials, including the American Protestant College—later the American University of Beirut—the American University of Cairo, and Roberts College in Istanbul, among others.

In Iran, unlike the Ottoman Empire, there were no missionary-sponsored institutions of higher education. However, the Presbyterians did establish some of the most modern and academically respected high schools in the country for both boys and girls. A few urban areas of the empire benefited from these educational facilities, and the best known of these schools was Alborz College in Tehran.

After several years of dedicated missionary work in Iran, Dr Jordan was appointed headmaster of the school. Under his long tenure, it became the most respected high school in the country, attracting the children of the elite and upper classes. It is also noteworthy that the Presbyterian school for girls, known as the American College, achieved similar success.

Because of his long years of service to Iranians, his personal charm, and his care for his students, Dr Jordan became an American icon to most educated Iranians. However, as Sattareh Farmanfarmaian observed, 'the point of [his] muscular Christianity was not lost on his Iranian students.'[144] The citizens of Tehran honoured him when they named one of the city's most attractive boulevards after him.

The End of an Era for Missionary Schools

In 1939, shortly after the start of war in Europe, the Iranian monarch, Reza Shah, ordered all foreign schools to be either closed or nationalised. The Ministry of Education took over administration of those schools. For Dr Jordan, that was the end of his Iranian journey, and he was forced to leave his beloved institutions. In October 1940, after spending more than 50 years in Iran, he and his wife returned to their homeland and settled in Pasadena.

Not surprisingly, when Helen, a Pasadena resident at the time, read in the newspapers that this highly respected and experienced American educator was to be the guest at one of the city's most prominent churches, she decided to attend the service. She and her husband were both eager to hear what he might say about Iran, the birthplace of Bahá'u'lláh.

After the formal service, the Bishops were surprised and rather astonished when the resident pastor asked his guest about the Bahá'í Faith in Iran. Both were bewildered when Dr Jordan responded: 'The Faith no longer exists in Iran.' He then went on to editorialise, adding, 'Bahá'ís were an insignificant eclectic group who even accepted atheists as believers in Bahá'u'lláh.'

Helen, never one to conceal her thoughts or emotions, challenged the speaker from the floor of the church: 'Sir, that is impossible.

Every page of Bahá'u'lláh's Book declares that God is; can Bahá'ís be atheists and still believe in God?'

Dr Jordan had not anticipated the presence of a 'believer' among the 'worshippers' at a crowded church in an affluent neighbourhood of Los Angeles. Lost for words, his only comment was that 'my colleague, Dr Wilson, has written the authoritative text on "Bahá'ísm."' The hush in the air demonstrated the congregation's uneasiness about the exchange.

Mrs Jordan, more composed than her husband, tried to intervene. She offered the explanation that her husband referred to 'Bahaism' as it was understood in Persia, whereas Helen was talking of it as it was promulgated in America! Helen thanked her for the attempt at reconciliation but pointed out that she discussed the Bahá'í Faith not from the perspective of an American Bahá'í, but from the Writings of Bahá'u'lláh:

> *I cannot accept the Teaching of Christ from hearsay—either secular or theological—but only from the Gospel ... how could Dr Wilson write his 'authoritative' text on the Bahá'í Faith without knowledge of Bahá'u'lláh's writings?*[145]

Then Dr Jordan dramatically left the rostrum, stood before Helen, and demanded to know what she found in Bahá'u'lláh's Teachings that she could not find in the Gospel. Helen replied:

> *Bahá'u'lláh gave the Law for nations.*[146]

The great missionary, perhaps recognizing that the subject was now beyond the frontiers of his knowledge or comprehension, said no more.

When the service was over, Helen, out of courtesy, went and shook the hand of Dr Jordan, 'because he had served in Bahá'u'lláh's native land.' As she was leaving the church, the pastor followed her and thanked her for being there and for asking questions. Helen replied:

I haven't much to say. I came to hear about Christian education in Iran. But I can say this: the world needs unity and any Faith that can meet the world's needs is the religion of tomorrow. That is all.[147]

Mrs Jordan offered her opinion that Iranian Bahá'ís were 'ignorant and superstitious' and that Helen should not be misguided by identifying them with the Bahá'ís in America! Helen then quietly asked:

Do you think you would have recognized Jesus as the Messiah if you had heard His Cause from the primitive and 'ignorant' Christians?[148]

Embarrassed, Mrs Jordan paused for few seconds and admitted that she supposed not. Helen agreed:

I think you would not have—just as you do.[149]

Then she asked to be excused and left the church.*

---

* Author's note: The account of the encounter between Helen and the Jordans is based on Helen's letter to the beloved Guardian, dated 14 April 1944. It is interesting to note that about the time that Dr Jordan was telling his American audience that the Bahá'í Faith no longer existed in Iran, I attended a religious service at an American chapel in Tehran in which, after the sermon, the minister–in response to someone's question about the Bahá'í Faith in America–replied with a straight face: 'The Bahá'í Faith does not exist in America!'

1944 : The Centennial Celebration

'Next month Mark [Tobey] and Charles and I shall be at our Centenary in Chicago (May 18-26),' Helen wrote to an English Bahá'í friend. 'It is to be the biggest event of our Bahá'í lives and I trust our mighty Lord sends us confirmation.'[150] It was, indeed, a time for celebration: the 100th anniversary of the Declaration of the Báb and the completion of their Seven-Year-Plan.

A Triumph Against the Odds

For the small but devoted Bahá'í community, the obstacles to overcome had been many. For five of the seven years, they, along with the rest of the world, endured the consequences of the most devastating war in history. The cost in human lives, cities, factories, farms, and properties—public and private—was incalculable. The liberation of Europe from German occupation by the Allied invasion of Normandy was still two months in the future, and victory over Germany and Japan was far from certain.

Achieving the Goals of the Seven-Year Plan

Yet, by the time of their annual convention in Chicago in 1944, and against all odds, North American Bahá'ís had fulfilled the objectives of the Seven-Year Plan. Between 1937 and 1944, the number of local spiritual assemblies in North America had risen from 72 to 136. In 1937, Bahá'ís resided in only 303 cities, but by 1944, that number had soared to 1,300. As planned, every state in the United States and every province in Canada had an established Bahá'í Assembly.

Internationally, their teaching goals were also met. Permanent assemblies had been formed in thirteen Latin American republics, as well as dependencies in the West Indies. The Guardian himself acknowledged that the expansion of the war into the Western Hemisphere had made the obstacles 'manifold and formidable.' However, he remained steadfast in his belief that 'the heroic self-sacrifice exhibited by the North American Bahá'í community' would enable them to overcome these challenges. And indeed, they had!

The Role of Pioneers in Latin America

The expansion of the Faith into Latin America was driven by the 'heroic self-sacrificing souls' who took up the call of Bahá'u'lláh. Figures such as Louise Caswell, Cora Oliver, Mrs H Emogene Hoagg, Mr and Mrs Ellsworth Blackwell, Elizabeth Cheney, Marcia Atwater, Josephine Kruka, Mathew Kaszab, Gerrard Slutter, and John Eichenauer played key roles in laying the foundations of the Bahá'í Faith in the region.

It is noteworthy that John Eichenauer, who pioneered in San Salvador in response to the call for service, was only seventeen years old—too young even to vote for or be elected to an assembly! Yet, his dedication exemplified the spirit of sacrifice and devotion that propelled the Faith's expansion.

Shoghi Effendi acknowledged their accomplishments, stating:

> ... the brilliant achievements of the heroic pioneers, the itinerant teachers, the indefatigable administrators of Bahá'í teaching activities, whether local, regional, or national, set the seal of total victory on the Seven Year Plan, befittingly consummate the fifty yearlong enterprises undertaken by the American Bahá'í community, and adorn the concluding chapter of the first Bahá'í century.[151]

The Completion of the House of Worship in Wilmette

Perhaps the most enduring legacy of the Centennial Celebration was the completion of the exterior ornamentation of the House of Worship in Wilmette. This magnificent edifice became a symbol of the majesty and splendour of the event, standing as an inspiration for generations to come.

Shoghi Effendi described the House of Worship in Wilmette as

> ... the most hallowed Temple ever to be erected by the followers of Bahá'u'lláh ... Neither the first Mashriqu'l-Adhkár of the Bahá'í world, reared in the city of 'Ishqábád,

nor any House of Worship to be raised in succeeding centuries, can claim to possess the vast, the immeasurable potentialities with which this Mother Temple of the West, established in the very heart of so enviable a continent, and whose foundation stone has been laid by the hand of the Center of the Covenant Himself, has been endowed. Conceived forty years ago by that little band of far-sighted and resolute disciples of 'Abdu'l-Bahá, members of the first Bahá'í community established in the Western Hemisphere; blessed and fostered by a vigilant Master Who directed its course from the hour of its inception to the last days of His life; supported by the spontaneous contributions of Bahá'ís poured in from the five continents of the globe, this noble, this mighty, this magnificent enterprise deserves to rank among the immortal epics that have adorned the annals of the Apostolic Age of the Faith of Bahá'u'lláh. [152]

A Temple of Light

During the annual Bahá'í Convention in 1920, held in New York City, six different designs were presented to the delegates for the House of Worship. Among them was a plaster model submitted by Louis Jean Bourgeois. The internationally renowned consulting architect, H Van Buren Magonigle, endorsed the selection, writing:

Mr. Bourgeois has conceived a Temple of Light in which the structure, as usually understood, is to be concealed, visible support eliminated as far as possible, and the whole fabric to take on the airy substance of a dream: it is a lacy envelope, enshrining an idea: the idea of Light, a shelter of cobweb imposed between earth and sky; struck through and through with light—light which shall partly consume the form and make it a thing of faery.[153]

A Historic Gathering in Wartime

The Guardian had called for an 'All-American Convention' to mark this very special occasion. Despite bureaucratic difficulties and strict wartime travel regulations, representatives from twelve Latin American republics managed to attend the historic event in Chicago.

Shoghi Effendi also instructed North American Bahá'ís to change the way they elected delegates to their annual convention. Previously, delegates had been chosen by local (municipal) communities through proportionate representation. However, by 1944, the number of local Bahá'í communities had grown so significantly that he felt the electorate should be expanded. 'All groups, all isolated believers, as well as local communities already possessing Assemblies, will henceforth share in the election of the Convention delegates,'[154] he directed. Thus, the area of representation was changed from the city to the state or province.

The First Statewide Conventions

Under the new method for electing delegates, California Bahá'ís held their first state convention on 9 April 1944 at the Ambassador Hotel in Los Angeles. They elected twenty-three delegates, including

Helen and Charles, who later attended the truly historic events from 19–24 May for the National Convention and the Centennial Celebration in Wilmette.

The Centennial Celebration itself was a loving and harmonious gathering of thousands representing many diverse nationalities, ethnic groups, and races. In the midst of a catastrophic global war, it stood as a testament to the creative power of a divinely ordained World Order. Throughout the Celebration, 'unity' was the recurring theme. Helen was among the main speakers, and on Sunday, 21 May, she spoke on the oneness of religion, sharing the platform with William Christian, who spoke on the oneness of humanity.

Reporting to the Guardian

After the convention, Helen wrote a comprehensive report of the Celebration for the Guardian, for which he expressed his deepest gratitude.

While preparing to go to Chicago for the convention, Helen had written to the Guardian, asking how she and Charles might best direct their services to the Faith in the future. The National Teaching Committee had suggested that everyone should go to a designated pioneering post, and Saskatchewan had been recommended for them. However, Helen strongly felt that many local spiritual assemblies around North America were in need of capable speakers to sustain the prestige of the Faith among an increasingly observant and critical public, including members of the press. 'Neither one of us,' she writes, 'can act without the sense of certainty ...'[155]

As soon as the convention ended, Helen sent her report to Shoghi Effendi and once again sought guidance on how best to serve now that the Seven-Year Plan had been completed. Rúḥíyyih Khánum responded on behalf of Shoghi Effendi:

The news of the great success which attended the Convention and celebration, as well as the unique spirit of love and unity prevailing the hearts of those present, has rejoiced his heart, and he feels that the Cause in America—north and south— has entered a new phase of development and will and must be brought to the attention of the general public as it never previously has been in the Western Hemisphere.[156]

In his own handwriting, the Guardian added:

Dear and valued co-workers; I wish ... [to] assure you of my keen and abiding appreciation of your continued services to our beloved Faith. I greatly value the spirit that animates you, and cherish great hopes for your future contribution to the consolidation of the institutions of our glorious Cause. I will continue to pray for your guidance and success from the depth of my heart. Your true and grateful brother, Shoghi.[157]

Rúḥíyyih Khánum added a postscript:

The Guardian would be very much pleased if you could go to Central America and aid in teaching work there. He suggests Central America as being nearer and perhaps less of strain on your health—but he leaves the choice to you.[158]

The Guardian's response was clear, and his suggestion of Central America was appropriate. Helen, with her deep knowledge of the language, culture, and people of the region, as well as her profound understanding of the spiritual and institutional aspects of the Faith, could contribute to the expansion and consolidation of the Faith in a way that few of her fellow Bahá'ís could.

The Decision to Pioneer

However, her husband Charles had reservations about pioneering. For Helen, the time had come to consider the unthinkable—pioneering without him.

She consulted with the Inter-America Committee, ruling out Nicaragua, Panama, and San Salvador due to her childhood experience with malaria. She suggested Montevideo, Uruguay, and considered taking a Bahá'í female friend as her companion so that she would not be travelling alone.[159]

As Helen and the committee explored the matter, they encountered logistical and bureaucratic challenges. The war was still ongoing, and Americans travelling to Latin America required passports and visas. Under Franklin Roosevelt's 'Good Neighbor Policy', the U.S. State Department was reluctant to issue passports for missionary work, though it remained a possibility. Helen, however, insisted that such a classification did not accurately reflect the purpose of her visit.

When the Inter-America Committee suggested she travel as a journalist, writing articles for World Order magazine or other non-Bahá'í publications, Helen rejected the idea immediately. She argued that it would be fraudulent since she had no intention of writing about anything other than the Faith.

Charles' Change of Heart

While consultations continued, an unexpected turn of events occurred. Charles, realising Helen's determination to go pioneering with or without him, changed his mind. He decided to accompany her, but this raised another issue: what visa classification could be used for his trip? Since Charles could not plausibly claim to be a journalist, the couple faced yet another bureaucratic challenge.

Helen was determined not to compromise the integrity of the Faith. She recalled that, during her pilgrimage to Haifa, Shoghi Effendi had expressed deep regret that some Persian Bahá'ís had misrepresented their reasons for travelling to Palestine, falsely claiming they were going for 'their health' !

A Direct Appeal to the U.S. Secretary of State

Determined to find a way forward, Helen took matters into her own hands. She wrote directly to US Secretary of State Edward Stettinius, Jr:

> *This is my application for a passport so that I may accompany my husband to the Caribbean Isles — more particularly Cuba, the Dominican Republic and Haiti. We hope to stay for a year. I affirm that our purpose in this visit is serious and necessary to our joint careers in making ties between peoples. For my own part, I view it as further preparation to carry on a responsible citizen's part in building the post war world. I am of a mind to use my training in the social sciences combined with a first hand knowledge of Spanish for research on the literature of Pan-Americanism. In a Spanish atmosphere, I can best read the Spanish texts pleading for a closer union of the Americas and prepare to interpret in my lectures to be given after my return to the States before the clubs, schools, churches and conferences I am accustomed to address…* [160]

Helen also sought support from her close Bahá'í friend, Sera Kenny, and her non-Bahá'í husband, Robert Kenny, who was then Attorney General of California. They agreed to serve as their identifying witnesses, while the Inter-America Committee became their official sponsor. At the time, Dorothy Baker chaired the committee, with Edna True as secretary. Other members included Amelia Collins, Loulie Mathews, and Philip Sprague.

A Waiting Game

As plans had changed, Helen contacted the National Spiritual Assembly to inform its members of the letter that she sent to the State Department. Horace Holley, secretary of the National Spiritual Assembly, suggested that:

> ... in the three Republics under consideration, Cuba, Haiti, and Dominican Republic, there were Bahá'í Groups though not deepened in the fundamental principles, or the institutions, of the Faith" and reminds Helen that "they needed a great deal of training and instructions.[161]

He further adds that the indigenous believers were to be reminded,

> ... to obey the civil authorities, not to participate in radical or subversive movements, and recognize that useful daily work was a form of worship. They were to be examples of lives devoted to the elimination of prejudice of race, creed, and class, and they were to be counseled not to be involved in the practice of psychic arts.[162]

Helen waited, but no personal response came from Secretary Stettinius. Given the timing, this was understandable—American troops were engaged in the Battle of the Bulge, and Stettinius was preparing to accompany President Roosevelt to Yalta for a pivotal meeting with Churchill and Stalin to redraw Europe's post-war map.

Chapter 5

FINDING HOME

Chapter 5

Concerns for Helen's Health

By the beginning of 1945, Helen's health had become a matter of concern for both her and her husband. 'No one will believe it,' she confesses in a letter to close friends Hope and Phil Thurmond in Portland, 'particularly when they see me on platform for an hour, but even household chores and social affairs must be planned for when one has become an utter softie.'[163] Her physical strength had noticeably declined, and she believed that a thorough medical examination was needed as her body ached for rest.

A Sojourn in Mexico

While awaiting a resolution regarding their plans for travel teaching in Central America, Helen and Charles decided to go to Mexico, where no passport was required. They informed the Inter-America Committee of their trip, and on 2 March 1945, they crossed the border and settled for three months in Mazatlán, where Helen's mother was born. 'It was very instructive for me to return with Charles and Madre,' she wrote, 'and to see what life had done to some friends. In that forgotten corner of the world we met persons who were as cultivated and high-minded as any that you may meet in the capitals of Europe.'[164]

It is interesting to note that in 1939, the Bishops had sent Helen's mother to her native Mexico for a visit, but her train was derailed by anarchists who thought the Mexican president was on board. Many were killed and wounded, and Helen's mother decided that it was a sign from heaven for her to return to her home in Portland.

Their stay in Mazatlán was not without its trials; both Helen and Charles suffered from infections caused by drinking the water. Despite this, Helen was able to speak publicly on several occasions about the Faith, and her talks received excellent reviews in the press. As was her custom, upon returning to the United States, she sent a detailed list of her contacts to the Inter-America Committee.

The Beloved Returns

For the centennial edition of The Bahá'í World, the Guardian asked Helen to contribute an appropriate article. As always, she obeyed and sent the manuscript to him. Shoghi Effendi was pleased with what he read and forwarded it to Horace Holley for publication in that special edition of *The Bahá'í World*. The article, titled 'The Beloved Returns,' begins:

> *For me there is something irrevocable about words in print and the sense of it halts my pen. A page should tell more about truth and lead to one of a thousand gates approaching*

> the Prophet. He is the Beloved One Whom we cannot know. Humanity is searching for Him, even while some humans unhappily defeat their own finding lest encounter with the Manifestation of Truth prove to be an end of opinions as well as the beginning of knowledge.[165]

In this beautifully crafted essay, Helen recounts how nine years before the war, while overseeing the Bahá'í Secretariat in Geneva, she attempted to present to the diplomats of the world an all-embracing plan for a World Community:

> ... the only Plan based upon the spiritual and organic relationships of nations, races, and religions; the only Plan divinely conceived, brought to earth by an Ambassador from Heaven.

She observed, however, that modern temper had:

> ... left religion out of the running, the only structural attempt to bring peace came through the League of Nations and was wholly secular ...Without benefit of Revelation, the League failed to create a new sense of collective consciousness binding a spiritual community of faith and law. The League had its esprit de corps, certainly, together with the excitement and hard work of its supporters throughout the world, but not a world-wide community dedicated to justice in the spiritual sense of Bahá'u'lláh's supplication: 'I beseech Thee by Thy Most Great Name to assemble them that love Thee around Thy Law.'[166]

She continues:

> *Bahá'u'lláh the 'Mighty Counselor' wrote to the kings and rulers to 'consider such ways and means as will lay the foundations of the world's Great Peace amongst men.' He commanded them to choose a universal auxiliary language, adopt a world-wide economic system, establish a World Court, and World Parliament, and constitute a World Police Force together with other institutions necessary to an emerging planetary culture rooted in the new awareness of the unity of man and of faith.' ... the World Reformer has come to transmute our natures by conferring a new grace and thereby to change our natural stations ... Under all His Names, past and present, the Bahá'ís love Him: for He is the Mediator. And He is the mystery of the Many and One. We love Him because He is the Beloved. Whenever we are not with Him we are engaged or even in conflict with duty, obedience, self-discipline, or sacrifice, but when we are with Him we are not at all aware of meeting those claims He puts upon us—we are aware only of Him. The Manifestation of God, the Beloved Who woos His creatures from themselves and to Himself. It is for this He returns.*[167]

Post-War Recovery and Alternative Medicine

The Second World War ended in August 1945 with the Japanese surrender to the Allies. Almost immediately, many wartime restrictions in the United States were lifted, including gas rationing. This made travel much easier, allowing the Bishops to attend the summer school at Geyserville. However, upon returning to Pasadena, Helen's sinus condition had worsened.

A friend, physicist Dimitri Marionoff, introduced her to his Russian acquaintance who would treat her with 'oxygen through the sound wave.' Helen, having always adhered to conventional medicine, now decided to explore alternative therapies. She admitted to Mark Tobey that she did a great deal of praying during the treatment, the details of which she did not fully understand, but she was encouraged by the fact that writer 'Aldous Huxley takes these treatments. He seems to understand them, I do not.'[168]

After four months of 'oxygen through sound' treatment from the Russian doctor, Helen's thyroid condition had not improved, though she did experience a general improvement in her overall health. Regardless of the treatment's effectiveness, Helen believed she was well enough to resume her activities on behalf of the beloved Cause.

1946: *The Second Seven Year Plan*

The 38th annual North American Bahá'í Convention was held in Wilmette in April 1946. Helen and Charles attended once again, elected as delegates from California. Helen described the 'golden hour' of the convention as the reading of Shoghi Effendi's message, which outlined the goals of the 'Second Seven Year Plan' for American Bahá'ís.

In his message, Shoghi Effendi urged the believers to construct a systematic and centered program to fulfill the objectives set by 'Abdu'l-Bahá in His Tablets of the Divine Plan. At the heart of these goals was the completion of the House of Worship in Wilmette, which would serve as the focal point of the celebration marking the 100th anniversary of Bahá'u'lláh's Revelation in the Síyáh-Chál prison:

> *The sacrifice demanded is such as to have no parallel whatsoever in the history of that community. The manifold issues inextricably interwoven with the campaign audaciously launched for the achievement of this high objective are of such a weighty character as to overshadow every enterprise embarked upon through the organized efforts of its members, in either the concluding years of the Heroic Age of the Faith or the first epoch of the Age which succeeded it ...*

He continues, quoting from Abdu'l-Bahá:

> *'A most wonderful and thrilling motion will appear in the world of existence,' are 'Abdu'l-Bahá's own words, predicting the release of spiritual forces that must accompany the completion of this most hallowed House of Worship. 'From that point of light,' He, further glorifying that edifice, has written, 'the spirit of teaching ... will permeate to all parts of the world.' And again: 'Out of this Mashriqu'l-Adhkár, without doubt, thousands of Mashriqu'l-Adhkárs will be born.' 'It marks the inception of the Kingdom of God on earth.'* [169]

Beyond completing the House of Worship, the plan called for the multiplication of Bahá'í centres and a bolder proclamation of the Faith to the masses. It also emphasized the formation of national assemblies in Canada, Central America, and South America. Additionally, American Bahá'ís were tasked with assisting their fellow believers in the 'Old World' by establishing at least one spiritual assembly each in Belgium, the Netherlands, Norway, Denmark, Sweden, Luxembourg, Switzerland, Italy, Portugal, and Spain.[170]

Helen's Unfiltered Reflections

While still in Wilmette, Helen promptly wrote and sent her delegate's report to the Bahá'ís of Pasadena. She explained that since she planned to embark on an extended teaching trip immediately after the convention, she did not want any delay in informing her Bahá'í friends of the historic event's highlights.

Helen's report was as forthright as her character. She expressed regret that, instead of consulting on the Guardian's soul-stirring cablegram, the delegates had spent 'two days discussing "procedure."' She lamented that such preoccupation with procedural details had hindered the Faith's expansion in North America. Otherwise, she reasoned, how else could one explain the fact that twenty-seven states had only one assembly each? Or that while Latin America had confirmed 130 new believers, only seventy had declared in the United States.[171]

A Joyful Reunion Through Letters

Despite her frustrations, Helen found immense joy in hearing news about the Bahá'ís in Europe—those cherished souls she had come to know and love while serving at the International Bahá'í Bureau in Geneva. During the war, she had remained in contact with British Bahá'í friends, but she had received no word regarding the German believers.

At the convention, she met Johnny Eichenhauver, a young pioneer in Latin America, who shared news and photographs of German Bahá'ís. Helen was deeply moved, especially seeing that they were 'smiling and solidly nourished by bread and spirit.' The pictures were especially touching because, as soon as the war ended, Helen and several American Bahá'ís had sent food and clothing packages to German believers.

One such package had gone to Edith Horn, Helen's pre-war travel-teaching companion. In a heartfelt letter, Frau Horn described the impact of these gifts:

> *The friends here are mostly unable to write in English, and too because of the many packages that were sent, we are acknowledging their receipt with this mimeographed letter. On one occasion we took a package to a Frau Brunning who was one of the first Bahá'ís in Frankfurt. She is quite elderly, suffers from chronic asthma, and is confined to bed that she has not been able to attend any of our meetings. She lives on the fifth floor of a shaky old apartment house which of course makes it all the more difficult for her. When we laid*

the coffee, dried milk, cheese, meat and other items of the package out on the bed, the tears began to flow from her eyes. She was so happy, we thought she was going to get out of bed and dance around the room. The material generosity of the American, Persian and Canadian Believers to the German Bahá'ís in this time of great hatred and prejudice, gives one a clear picture of what our future world will be like when all souls are united in true love and harmony ... Our love goes out to the Bahá'ís everywhere, whom we love as our brothers and sisters. We feel your love and the unity of this great World Faith growing stronger each day. We have every confidence in the prophecies that soon all mankind will be overtaken by the overflowing power, love and light of the Holy Spirit.[172]

Around the same time, Helen also received a letter from her New York Bahá'í friends, Rafi and Mildred Mottahedeh. Having recently visited Great Britain, they shared that many British Bahá'ís, particularly in Manchester, inquired about her and expressed their gratitude for her past services. Rafi planned to return to England and asked if Helen had any messages for her friends there. She responded:

[Please tell them] that I with a new surge of life and energy [am] en route to Convention and on a three month tour ... On Canadian soil I shall think steadfastly of England and entrust the rays of love with the Master, who said that it was impossible for us to gauge the far-reaching influences of the power of the Kingdom. Every one of the friends appear vividly before us: Captain Baker, Hasan Balyuzi and his wife and her mother, Rosalind, Dorothy Ferraby, Mrs. George,

Mary Basil Hall, the Nortons, the Coopers, the Persians of Manchester, and the wonderful believers of Torquay, besides Marion and David Hofman. May God bless them.[173]

A New Mission: Pioneering in Canada

The Guardian's plan called for Canada to establish its own National Spiritual Assembly. While Helen and Charles had originally intended to pioneer in Latin America, circumstances made that impossible. Instead, they turned to Canada—a land they loved and where they had many dear friends.

Writing to the National Teaching Committee, they proposed a three-month travel-teaching journey across the country. They visited Winnipeg, Regina, Calgary, Edmonton, Vernon, Vancouver, and Victoria. In each city, with the help of local Bahá'ís, they organized public meetings and firesides that received positive press coverage. Helen later wrote to the Guardian:

Bahá'ís have welcomed us and provided the avenues for meeting individuals and groups in line ... The response has been so overwhelming that both Charles and I have intimations that the Cause will make a forward stride in this magnificent country.[174]

Upon returning to the United States, they continued their travel-teaching in the southeast and southwest, reaching many Spanish-speaking communities. However, constant travel at their advanced age made them yearn for a settled life. Helen wrote to the National Teaching Committee, asking for guidance:

> … *establish our residence in an area favorable for the work of the Second Seven Year Plan. Naturally, we prefer to go to a state having as yet only one Assembly, and to a town without an Assembly, but we realize the housing shortage throughout the country is still so acute that we may not find it possible to settle precisely where we wish.* [175]

At the National Teaching Committee's request, the Bishops visited Salt Lake City, where Marguerite and William Sears had been homefront pioneering for a number of years. The small yet devoted Bahá'í community made full use of their presence. William interviewed Helen over the radio and Helen spoke at a well-attended Christmas gala on 'Peace at Christmas, Peace of Mind, Peace among Nations.' A representative of the state governor, during the dinner conversation, told Helen that he had read Shoghi Effendi's *The Promised Day Is Come* (no doubt a gift from the Sears!) but made no comments about it.

His Japanese Witnesses

Shortly before Helen and Charles left for Utah, Helen received a letter from the beloved Guardian suggesting that she draft an article for the forthcoming edition of *The Bahá'í World*.[176] The choice of subject was clear to Helen. The previous summer, while attending the Geyserville Bahá'í School with Charles and their close friend, Mark Tobey, she had been deeply engaged in reading the nineteen Tablets that 'Abdu'l-Bahá had addressed to Japanese Bahá'ís.

Helen had first encountered these Tablets years earlier while on her honeymoon in Hawai'i. However, as she later admitted, at the time, the Japanese people were an enigma to her. Everything changed in 1945 when the atomic bomb was dropped on Japan, and those letters by 'Abdu'l-Bahá took on a profound new significance. She proposed to Charles and Mark that they study the Tablets through the lens of world events.

During their discussions, she recalled a striking moment from 1911 when 'Abdu'l-Bahá, while in Paris, met the Japanese Ambassador to Spain, Viscount Arawaka, at Hotel d'Jena. In their conversation, the Master had warned:

> *Scientific discoveries have increased material civilization. There is in existence a stupendous force, as yet happily undiscovered by man. Let us supplicate God, the beloved, that this force be not discovered by science until spiritual civilization shall dominate the human mind. In the hands of men of lower material nature, this power would be able to destroy the whole earth.*[177]

The Japanese Bahá'ís and Their Destiny

The first of these Tablets was written in 1916 to a young Japanese student—the first Japanese believer on native soil to bear witness to Bahá'u'lláh. Seven of the Tablets were addressed to schoolgirls in Tokyo, while five were written to blind young men who, despite their physical blindness, had 'found the true Light of this New Day.' The final Tablet, written in November 1921—the month of 'Abdu'l-Bahá's Ascension—recognized 'new friends in Korea.' In it, He made a powerful statement:

> In Japan the divine proclamation will be heard as a formidable explosion, so that those who are ready will become uplifted and illumined by the Light of the Sun of Truth.[178]

Helen's Reflections : Understanding the Japanese Soul

In her article *His Japanese Witnesses*, Helen wrote that 'Abdu'l-Bahá

> ... did understand the Japanese. He knew them—as He knew all children of the Most High God. One sees the child not as he is, but knows the child is as he will be. And that is how 'Abdu'l-Bahá foresaw the destiny of a people and paid us all attribute to the spirituality of the Japanese.[179]

She quoted from one of 'Abdu'l-Bahá's letters to a young girl in Tokyo:

> The people of Japan are like unto a soil that has been deprived of rain for centuries and generations and has

no share of the outpouring of rain and even a dew ... Such a soil as this has great capacity. One seed produces a hundredfold.[180]

Helen believed that even a small group of devoted Bahá'ís in Japan could transform the entire nation, as Bahá'u'lláh's power was always at work:

It lies within the offices of the Holy Spirit to make captive of us all—not all at once, but just a few at the beginning and these distributed among the nations. Resistance and ambivalence notwithstanding, the love of God is going to dominate mankind ... We will claim that a world-wide acceptance of Bahá'u'lláh would work for a spiritual change within outwards whilst His divine plan for one World Community is now at work from without inwards. And that all lesser planning will break down because either the inner or the outer change is wanting.[181]

Mark Tobey : A Lifelong Friend and Renowned Artist

Helen had first met Mark Tobey in 1933 when she travelled to Europe as director of the Bahá'í International Bureau. Mark had been pioneering in Great Britain since 1931. Later, he met Charles, and the three became lifelong friends.

Born in 1890 in Wisconsin, Mark began his artistic career as a commercial artist in New York in 1912. In 1917, at the age of 27, he held his first solo exhibition at M. Knoedler & Co. His travels to Mexico and the Far East influenced his work, particularly his studies of Chinese calligraphy and Japanese brushwork. These inspirations shaped his unique artistic style, which art historians recognized as a significant contribution to contemporary art.

His artistic genius was acknowledged by major institutions, including the Museum of Modern Art in New York. In 1958, he won the prestigious Leone d'Oro at the Venice Biennale, becoming the first American since Whistler to receive that honour. In 1974, his paintings were featured in a major exhibition at the National Collection of Fine Arts at the Smithsonian Institution. The Louvre in Paris even extended him an unprecedented invitation to present a retrospective of his work at the Musée des Arts Décoratifs—an honour never before granted to a living American artist.[182]

A New Dawn After the Devastation of War

Helen concluded her reflections with optimism. The dawn of a new age—signalled by the unprecedented destructive power unleashed on Hiroshima and Nagasaki—would also serve as a step closer to humanity's ultimate destiny: the unification of all the children of God. She believed the process had already begun with the ratification of the Charter of the United Nations in San Francisco that same year.

Her unwavering faith in the transformative power of Bahá'u'lláh's message affirmed that, despite the trials of war and destruction, the seeds of a spiritually unified world had already begun to take root.

1948 : For the Faith—Two Great Triumphs

Canada's National Spiritual Assembly

In 1948, Canadian Bahá'ís achieved a significant milestone by electing their own National Spiritual Assembly. This made Canada the youngest of the nine National Spiritual Assemblies that existed worldwide at the time.

United Nations Recognition of the Bahá'í Faith

That same year, the Bahá'í Faith received an unexpected but momentous recognition on the international stage. The United States government submitted an application to the United Nations, requesting official recognition of the Bahá'í Faith as an international non-governmental body. The petition was accepted, and the UN formally recognized the National Spiritual Assembly of the United States as the representative of all other Bahá'í National Spiritual Assemblies. This entitled the Bahá'í community to send representatives to various UN conferences.

Shoghi Effendi described this development as an:

> ... *important step forward in the struggle for our beloved Faith to receive in the eyes of the world its just due and be recognized as an independent World Religion. Indeed, this step should have a favorable reaction in the program of the Cause everywhere, especially on those parts of the world*

where it is still persecuted, belittled, or scorned, particularly in the East.[183]

For Helen, the elevation of the Faith's status in the international community was a remarkable transformation. When she assumed the directorship of the International Bahá'í Bureau in Geneva in 1933, the League of Nations did not legally recognize it as a formal bureau. As a result, its influence and effectiveness were limited. However, under the United Nations Charter, the situation changed significantly.

In May 1948, three distinguished Bahá'ís—Ugo Giachery, Mason Remey, and Mildred Mottahedeh—were officially recognized as Bahá'í representatives. This recognition granted them the ability to attend and actively participate in the sessions of a major UN conference for international non-governmental organizations, held in Geneva.*

The Bahá'í Faith had taken another step forward on the global stage, solidifying its presence in international discourse and expanding its influence as a recognized and independent world religion.

---

* Author's note: Marion Holley and Leroy Ioas were also appointed but were unable to serve.

A Home at Last !

Helen wrote to Shoghi Effendi, sharing her thoughts about their travels and her deep longing for a permanent home:

> *Be sure that we did not pass by casually your proposal that we extend our travels into the Latin America field ... the [Inter America] Committee did not approve when I offered to go to Montevideo without [Charles] a year ago ...*

> *Meanwhile, I have been active locally desiring with all my heart that we can establish a permanent home somewhere, leaving it from time to time to accomplish our joint mission in many parts of the Bahá'í World Community. When it comes to the Cause, dear, dear Guardian, my morale is high.*[184]

Since their return from Europe in 1937, the Bishops had lived without a permanent home, using rented houses as bases for their travel-teaching efforts. In response to their unwavering dedication, Shoghi Effendi expressed his deep appreciation, writing to them:

> *... for the great services rendered the Cause of Bahá'u'lláh in so many ways and over so many years ... which have been invariably of real and much needed assistance to the centers you have visited.*[185]

Return to Portland

By the late 1940s, Helen recognized that their constant travel had taken a toll on Charles, who was now over 60 years old. The wear of two decades of near-constant motion had affected his health. In April 1950, still in Southern California, they moved from their rented house to a studio apartment, preparing for a more settled life. Both agreed, however, that their final home would not be in California. It was time to return to Portland.

That summer, they made their way back to the beautiful city by the Willamette River, searching for a house to call their own.

Finding Their Dream Home

On the night of 2 August 1950, Helen recorded a vivid dream in her diary:

> *Dream of the half-brick house in a dark night; the windows showed the house was ablaze with light.*

The very next day, a real estate agent showed Helen and Charles a house on 24th Street, and Helen immediately recognized it—it was the house from her dream. Built in 1912, the same year of 'Abdu'l-Bahá's visit to the United States, the home featured four bedrooms, two baths, two fireplaces, exquisite wood panelling, and beautiful hardwood floors.

For the real estate agent, the sale was almost immediate. By 15 August, Charles had placed an earnest deposit, and by 24 August, the deed was officially recorded. At last, the Bishops had a home of their own.

To Helen, the house carried mystical and spiritual significance from the very beginning. She noted in her diary that it would 'become a new basis for service.' The day after moving in, when their dear friend Marzieh Gail visited, she suggested that their home should serve as the *hazirah* of Portland.

A Sacred Space for the Faith

Helen recorded another special moment in her diary:

> *Tonight for the first time we returned to the house after dinner ... lighted three candles and recited mighty Prayer of Names.*

On 6 December, she reflected on their transition from years of travel to finally settling down:

> *Strange to some that we have come down to domesticity after our travels, but the sense of purpose does not find it strange. The home is our Center.*[186]

The first Bahá'í Feast they hosted in their new home was the Feast of Masa'il (Questions). Helen felt that this event had consecrated their home, writing:

The house has broken its ties with the past. It is entirely ours. We can use it for the work of Heaven.

An Honoured Visit

In May 1953, their home received a profound blessing. Two Hands of the Cause of God, Rúḥíyyih Khánum and Jináb-i-Samandarí, visited the Bishops. Helen was overjoyed and recorded her emotions in her diary:

Tonight our happiness is complete. This is an honor for this house, for Charles and me—my family—and our community and this city. For the Heart and Head of our Great Cause is in the Holy Land, but the Hands are here tonight. And now you all share our happiness and we are in their Hands.[187]

The Bishops' home had become more than just a place of residence—it was a sacred space, a centre for service, and a source of joy for the Baháʼí community.

'Introduction' to the Book of Certitude

As the Bishops planned for their 'more settled life,' Helen received an extraordinary honour from the National Spiritual Assembly of the United States. She was asked to write the introduction for the new edition of the Book of Certitude (Kitáb-i-Íqán), Bahá'u'lláh's profound work on the principle of progressive revelation.

Shoghi Effendi had translated the Kitáb-i-Íqán into English in 1931, and it was first published in the United States that same year. By 1950, a new edition was planned, and the National Assembly felt that an explanation of its significance—especially for Western readers—was necessary.

Helen was deeply moved by the request, but she also recognized the weight of the responsibility. She recorded in her diary:

> It has absorbed my soul and mind ... [188]

True to her steadfast obedience to the institutions of the Faith, she accepted the challenge. By 23 November 1949, she had completed the seventeen-page manuscript and sent it to the Bahá'í Publishing Trust.

Explaining the Essence of the Kitáb-i-Íqán

Helen's introduction eloquently summarized the principle of progressive revelation as revealed by Bahá'u'lláh. She explained how Bahá'u'lláh confirmed the divine origins of Judaism, Christianity, and Islam, and she highlighted the Báb's two-fold station—as both the forerunner of the World Redeemer and as a Prophet in the lineage of Abraham.

However, Helen emphasized that implicit within *The Book of Certitude* was the Station of Bahá'u'lláh Himself:

> *The Prophets are the standards for man's knowledge of God: all religious truth has its root in Their Revelation ... The Manifestation is the embodiment of the First Principle, which is the Effulgence of the Holy Spirit proceeding from the indivisible Essence of God ... The Manifestation is the Reflection of the Holy Spirit—the shining and moving Reality that can be known by all men ... They can be named and Their station differentiated in terms of Personality, time, and rank, but in the essential unity of the Divine Spirit, the Many are become the One.*[189]

She also explored a major theme in the Book of Certitude—the 'clouds' that obscure the Sun of Truth from reaching humanity:

> *The Word is the Bearer of the Spirit that restores and redeems the soul. Man is dwarfed whenever he is deprived of its bestowals. And yet deprived man will be — if the clergy stands between the seeker and the divine light.*[190]

Helen's introduction remained part of all subsequent editions of the Book of Certitude until after the passing of Shoghi Effendi, when the Universal House of Justice later decreed that the Holy Texts of the Faith should be published without any accompanying commentary.

Helen's Studies of Judaism

Although establishing a home in Portland naturally altered the Bishops' lifestyle, service to the Faith remained their highest priority. They continued to attend Bahá'í summer schools, conventions, and special events whenever possible, and Helen was still in great demand as a speaker. However, they had to place some limits on their travels.

Their more settled life also allowed Helen to pursue new studies that she had long desired to undertake. One such pursuit was a more systematic and thorough study of Judaism.

During her visit with the Guardian in 1934, Shoghi Effendi had encouraged Helen to study the Jewish Faith. She had always admired Jewish history and traditions, but she now had the opportunity to explore them in greater depth.

While writing her introduction to the Book of Certitude, she reflected on the historic events unfolding around her. The State of Israel was being established, and she recorded her thoughts:

> *Israel is precious to Bahá'u'lláh because of its kinship with the Prophets through Whom is our salvation. Jewish history gives the plainest lesson in the rhythm of a Prophet's challenge, and a people's response to the Light. The divine Truth-telling is forever the rally to greatness. Israel was rightly named God's Champion—the transmitter of monotheism and preserver from idolatry amid the nations.*[191]

As she rejoiced in the Jewish people's homecoming, she wrote that for Jews:

> ... there can be no home-coming more glorious than meeting with The Father of mankind and fraternity in the world-wide community of the Most Great Name.[192]

Helen actively sought opportunities to learn from Jewish scholars and religious leaders. She attended study classes at Portland synagogues and developed friendships with some of the city's most distinguished rabbis.

In two letters to the Guardian (21 August and 9 September 1951), she shared her progress in Jewish studies. In response, Shoghi Effendi's secretary wrote on his behalf, encouraging her to continue her studies and dialogue. The letter also assured her:

> ... any friends of yours that care to see the Shrines and Gardens here, would be most welcome and that arrangements will be made for their visits.[193]

Helen maintained her deep connection with the Jewish community of Portland for the rest of her life. She was honoured by them on several occasions, including in October 1957, when she was presented with a gold pin at a private tea party in Portland as a sponsor of Israeli bonds.

Chapter 6

LATTER YEARS

Chapter 6

The Inauguration of the Ten-Year World Crusade

From 29 April to 6 May 1953, American Bahá'ís commemorated the centenary of Bahá'u'lláh's Revelation in the Síyáh-Chál with a grand jubilee. The event coincided with the 45th Annual Bahá'í Convention, during which Rúḥíyyih Khánum delivered a powerful message from the Guardian.

Shoghi Effendi's message began with words of triumph:

> *My soul is uplifted in joy and thanksgiving at the triumphant conclusion of the second Seven Year Plan, immortalized by the brilliant victories simultaneously won by the vanguard of the hosts of Bahá'u'lláh in Latin America, in Europe and in Africa—victories crowned through the consummation of a fifty year old enterprise, the completion of the first Mashriqu'l-Adkár of the western world.*[194]

He described the 'administrative exploits unparalleled in the annals of any Bahá'í National Community whether in the East or in the West,' and offered a 'warmest tribute' to the American Bahá'ís, who had played a 'pre-eminent share' in numerous historic milestones:

> ... *proclaiming Bahá'u'lláh's Revelation, in shielding His Cause, in championing His Covenant, in erecting the administrative machinery of His embryonic World Order, in expounding His teachings, in translating and disseminating His Holy Word, in dispatching the messengers of His Glad-Tidings, in awakening Royalty to His Call, in succoring His oppressed followers, in routing His enemies, in upholding His Law, in asserting the independence of His Faith, in multiplying the financial resources of its nascent institutions and, the last but not the least, in rearing its Greatest House of Worship.*[195]

A Historic Gathering in Wilmette

Helen and Charles Bishop were among those present when the magnificent House of Worship in Wilmette opened its doors to visitors and delegates. The scale of the event was awe-inspiring. On the first day alone, more than 1,700 Bahá'ís gathered. By the end of the week, 2,300 Bahá'ís from thirty-three different countries had registered for the historic occasion.

After electing permanent officers for the Convention, the attendees welcomed six Hands of the Cause of God from Persia:

- Valiyu'lláh Varqá
- Tarazu'lláh Samandarí
- Ali Akbar Furútan
- Dhikru'lláh Khádem
- General Shua'u'lláh Alá'í
- Musá Banání

The Secretary of the National Spiritual Assembly presented a remarkable report: all four goals of the second Seven Year Plan had been accomplished. These included:

1. The opening of ten goal countries in Europe, with nineteen Local Spiritual Assemblies established.

2. The completion of the Wilmette Temple.

3. The formation of three new National Spiritual Assemblies in the Americas—one in Canada and two in Latin America.

4. The consolidation and proclamation of the Faith in the United States.

By 1953, the recent formation of the Italo-Swiss National Spiritual Assembly had brought the number of National Spiritual Assemblies to twelve—key pillars in the development of the Universal House of Justice.

A Sacred Dedication and Worldwide Recognition

On Friday 1 May a private consecration service for Bahá'ís was held, commemorating 'Abdu'l-Bahá's 1912 visit to the site of the House of Worship. The following day, 3,600 people attended the public dedication across three consecutive services. An estimated 1,500 additional attendees were unable to enter due to capacity limits.

The event drew international recognition, with messages of support from prominent global figures, including:

- Abba Eban, Israel's Ambassador to the United States
- Charles Malik, Lebanese Ambassador to the United States
- Ruth Bryan Rohde, former U.S. Ambassador to Denmark
- William O Douglas, US Supreme Court Justice

Many dignitaries who could not attend sent cablegrams, letters, and congratulatory notes.

Dr Paul R Anderson, President of the Pennsylvania College for Women, wrote:

I have never met more serious believers in the cause of humanity than Bahá'ís. Such loyalty to the highest ideals is what we need to bring us closer to the goal of a peaceful, friendly world. [196]

Dr Marcus Bach of the State University of Iowa reflected:

While the dedication of your House of Worship symbolizes this fact in ceremonial, it remains for true followers of the Glory of God to instill its principle in the hearts of men. The words of Bahá'u'lláh, which have become a challenge and a working formula for our time, have long been my text, 'The earth is but one country; and mankind its citizens.' These words, strengthened by my recent visit with the Guardian, are now further intensified by the rising influence demonstrated in the Intercontinental Centenary Conferences. [197]

Dr Raymond Piper of Syracuse University's Philosophy Department sent this message:

The Bahá'í House of Worship is a unique and magnificent achievement in the history of the world's religions and cultures because it embodies, in incomparable, compelling, and unforgettable beauty, the glorious ideal of the enlightened and creative unity of religions, and also because it is a sun-clear, enduring symbol which invites all religionists, and others too, to work together in loving sympathy for the sake of multiplying those precious fruits of goodwill, wisdom, peace, and joy of which mankind now stands in profound and painful need.[198]

Voices of Civil Rights Leaders

Particularly notable were the messages from two distinguished African Americans who represented the National Association for the Advancement of Colored People (NAACP)—the renowned civil rights organization that 'Abdu'l-Bahá had addressed in 1912.

Roy Wilkins, chief administrator of the NAACP, wrote to the National Spiritual Assembly:

I am happy to send greetings to the members of the Bahá'í Faith and their friends upon the occasion of dedication of your temple to the brotherhood of man. Our poor world is in great need of the deep faith and sincere unostentatious practices of the Bahá'ís.[199]

Thurgood Marshall, then director and counsel for the NAACP's Legal and Educational Fund (and later a US Supreme Court Justice), sent this cablegram:

> *We are happy to extend greetings and best wishes on the occasion of the dedication of the Bahá'í House of Worship. You affirmatively offer full religious fellowship to all without the distinction based upon race and color and are thereby attempting to put into practice one of the highest ideals of religious and democratic teachings. Our organization is dedicated to the same end although through the use of different tools. We are, therefore, fellow-soldiers trying to build a society in which there will be no place for distinction and differences based upon race, color, class, or religion.*[200]

A Monumental Step Forward

The dedication of the House of Worship in Wilmette marked a profound milestone for the Bahá'í Faith, not only as a sacred edifice but also as a beacon of unity and peace. The event reinforced the Faith's growing influence worldwide, bringing together leaders, scholars, and civil rights advocates in a collective vision of hope for humanity.

For Helen and Charles Bishop, witnessing this historic occasion was a culmination of decades of service, reinforcing their lifelong dedication to Bahá'u'lláh's Cause.

The Ten-Year Plan

The 1953 Jubilee marked a celebration of the Bahá'í Faith's first hundred years, but it also signified the beginning of a new journey. On 3 May 1953, Shoghi Effendi, in his message to the All-America Conference, described the gathering as:

> *... the most momentous gathering held since the close of the Heroic Age of the Faith and will be regarded as the most potent agency in paving the way for the launching of the most brilliant phases of the greatest crusade ever undertaken by the followers of Bahá'u'lláh since the inception of His Faith more than a hundred years ago.* [201]

At the Forty-Fifth Annual Bahá'í Convention of the United States, Shoghi Effendi outlined his vision for the Faith's future. He called upon the American Bahá'í community to reaffirm its leadership by launching a new spiritual campaign—the Ten-Year Plan.

This Plan, which he described as the third and final stage of the initial epoch in the evolution of 'Abdu'l-Bahá's Master Plan, had a bold and global scope:

> *The hour is ripe for the greatly gifted, richly blessed Community to arise and reaffirm, through the launching of yet another enterprise, its primacy, enhance its spiritual heritage, plumb greater depth of consecration and capture loftier heights in the course of its strenuous and ceaseless labors for the exaltation of God's Cause.* [202]

Shoghi Effendi clarified that the ultimate goal of the Ten-Year Plan was:

> ... the conquest of the citadels of men's hearts. The theater of its operations is the entire planet. Its duration is a whole decade. Its commencement synchronizes with the centenary of the birth of Bahá'u'lláh's Mission. Its culmination will coincide with the centenary of the declaration of that same Mission.[203]

He called upon Bahá'ís to pioneer in regions where the Faith had not yet been established. Those who accomplished this were designated as Knights of Bahá'u'lláh, and their names were inscribed in a Roll of Honour.

Inspired by the Guardian's call, the National Spiritual Assembly of the United States created the US Africa Teaching Committee, chaired by Elsie Austin. Among its members was Amoz Gibson, who would later be elected to the Universal House of Justice at its first election in 1963.

Each of the twelve National Spiritual Assemblies worldwide was assigned specific goals for the decade-long Plan. The US Africa Teaching Committee had four key objectives:

1. Training Bahá'í pioneers to effectively teach and establish the Faith.

2. Placing American Bahá'í pioneers in designated African goal territories.

3. Surveying opportunities for Bahá'í expansion in Africa.

4. Encouraging Bahá'í communities in America to engage with and teach African students in the US

The Global Context : A World in Turmoil

The 1950s was a turbulent decade. While the Bahá'í Faith was embarking on a global expansion, humanity faced unprecedented challenges. The world was grappling with:

- The Korean War (1950–1953), a conflict fuelled by Cold War tensions.
- The rise of nuclear weapons, as both the United States and the Soviet Union developed hydrogen bombs and intercontinental ballistic missiles.
- Colonial uprisings in Africa and Asia, as nations fought for independence from European powers.
- Political unrest in Eastern Europe, with Hungarians, Germans, and Poles resisting Soviet-backed regimes.
- The escalation of the Vietnam conflict, which would later draw the United States into its longest war.
- The Arab-Israeli conflict, which had begun in 1948 and continued to destabilize the region.
- The Cuban Missile Crisis (1962), a confrontation that nearly led to nuclear war between the United States and the Soviet Union.

Amid this chaos, Bahá'ís worldwide remained steadfast, dedicating themselves to the Faith's expansion and responding enthusiastically to Shoghi Effendi's call.

The Bishops' Role in the Ten-Year Plan

Helen and Charles Bishop returned home from the Jubilee celebrations deeply inspired. Although their circumstances prevented them from pioneering, they actively supported the Plan through travel-teaching, both in the US and abroad. They travelled to East Asia, visiting Bahá'ís and seekers in Korea, China, and Japan, and were profoundly moved by the Faith's expansion in the region.

The impact of the Ten-Year Plan was extraordinary:

- In 1953, there were 12 National Spiritual Assemblies. By 1963, that number had grown to 56.
- The Plan had aimed for 5,000 Bahá'í localities worldwide. By 1963, there were over 13,000.
- At the outset of the Plan, the majority of Bahá'ís were Iranian. By the end of the Plan there was a diverse worldwide community.

Conclusion : A Historic Transformation

The Ten-Year Plan was a defining period for the Bahá'í Faith. Despite the challenges of a rapidly changing world, the Bahá'í community flourished, fulfilling Shoghi Effendi's vision and laying the groundwork for the establishment of the Universal House of Justice.

For Helen and Charles Bishop, participating in this momentous expansion reinforced their lifelong devotion to Bahá'u'lláh's Cause. Their travels, experiences, and commitment contributed to the Faith's remarkable growth, helping to shape the future of the global Bahá'í community.

The Passing of the Guardian

The masterful architect of the Ten-Year Plan, Shoghi Effendi, passed away unexpectedly in November 1957 while in London, having suffered from Asian flu. At just 60 years old, his sudden passing deeply shocked the Bahá'í world. The Hands of the Cause of God sent out a cable announcing the tragic news, rallying the community to ensure that all of the Guardian's goals would still be met.

By April 1963, the Faith had fifty-six National Spiritual Assemblies. Representatives from these diverse communities gathered in Haifa for the first election of the Universal House of Justice—the institution Shoghi Effendi had described as the 'Apex of the Bahá'í Administrative Order'[204] and 'the Supreme Organ of the Bahá'í Commonwealth'[205] and 'the last refuge for a tottering civilization.'[206]

For those, like Helen and Charles Bishop, who had known Shoghi Effendi personally, his loss was devastating. Helen never fully recovered from the deep sense of personal grief. Nearly 30 years later, in

1985, it was suggested that Helen visit the Holy Land to witness how the Guardian had transformed Mount Carmel into the Mountain of God. Her response was immediate and poignant:

> *I cannot even imagine returning to Haifa where Shoghi Effendi is there no more.*[*]

The First World Bahá'í Congress (1963)

In 1963, the Bahá'í world celebrated the Centenary of Bahá'u'lláh's Declaration at the First World Bahá'í Congress in London's Albert Hall. Thousands of Bahá'ís from around the world attended, witnessing the remarkable expansion of the Faith in just a single century.

Shoghi Effendi had once observed that one of 'Abdu'l-Bahá's greatest accomplishments was transforming 'subjective faith into positive cooperative action.'[207]

By the time 'Abdu'l-Bahá passed away in 1921, the World Order of Bahá'u'lláh had been defined but not fully established—it existed as a blueprint. Under Shoghi Effendi's leadership, that blueprint became a living organism, as the rudimentary administrative institutions developed into a fully functioning global system of governance.

---

* The suggestion was posed by the author and his wife.

Helen and Charles : Dedicated Travel-Teachers

Between 1892 and 1963, the American Bahá'í community had grown dramatically—from just over 1,000 believers to more than 100,000. While this expansion was a cause for celebration, some older Bahá'ís, like Helen, missed the intimacy of earlier times.

Despite the changing nature of the Bahá'í community, Helen and Charles remained dedicated teachers. In 1966, a year before Charles passed away, Helen's journal reveals an ambitious travel-teaching journey. Traveling 'north by car,' they visited Iowa, Nebraska, Texas, Kansas, Oklahoma, New Mexico, Arizona, and California. Helen addressed a philosophy class of 300 students at the University of Oklahoma, where over 200 students took Bahá'í literature. She lectured at the Universities of New Mexico, Northern Arizona, and Texan Western. At Odessa College, Texas, known for having the highest number of John Birch Society members per capita (members of a radically conservative society), she was the first person to mention Bahá'u'lláh by name on campus. She was interviewed on NBC Radio in Lubbock, Texas. In Albuquerque, New Mexico, she received the best newspaper coverage of the entire trip.[208]

Helen was deeply moved by the enthusiastic response she received, particularly from college students.

Charles' Passing

Soon after their travel-teaching tour, Charles Bishop passed away on 9 July 1967. The Universal House of Justice sent a cablegram, calling his passing

> ... *a great loss to the whole Bahá'í world.* [209]

Helen was devastated. Their marriage had been a spiritual as well as physical union, despite their contrasting personalities. Helen, vivacious and outspoken, had found balance and peace in Charles, who was quiet and contemplative. She once wrote:

> *Charles' temperament does not precipitate antagonism, mine does. It also precipitates the decision that makes me a teacher or one who transmits the Word for men to accept or reject.* [210]

In a letter to a Canadian friend, she reflected:

> *All other activities tear me to pieces unless I have an inner peace, and that I can maintain spending some hours away from people (yet with Charles) reading Tablets or doing quiet non-mental work sewing.* [211]

As Honor Kempton explained it once:

> *I can not tell you how much I am longing to see you and to hear Charles' quiet voice which seems to tell you everything is all right ...* [212]

Of her marriage, in a letter to a friend in England, Helen wrote:

> *I dare say I am persuaded on behalf of marriage, because ours is a blessed one ... it is made in the Cause and will advance its claim upon them and all those who live in their orbit. That is right and good, isn't it?*[213]

The National Spiritual Assembly of the United States sent a gracious letter of condolence to Helen. It was not just a formal letter of recognition of Charles' many years of devoted service to his beloved Cause, but also an expression of deep love and sorrow that each member felt since each knew him personally and intimately as a friend. Helen wrote to Charlotte Linfoot, then the assistant secretary of the Assembly:

> *... I am undone by kindness ... From all sides I am overwhelmed by expression of admiration or love for Charles, and sorrow for me ... Gone from our sight and hearing and touch. Yet when I am alone, the Great Words resound within like an interior breathing. I see Charles' immortal image together with you or Horace [Holley], Mark [Tobey], George [Latimer], Catherine True or somebody, all companions of the path. And when I am alone, I do not cry ... I am praising God for Charles' long life; really the last ten years were bestowal. 'One is young a very long time, Helen,' he said, 'Now I have grown old' ... Charles' head was on her arms [those of Frances Grandy, Helen's sister] while I was preparing him for the ambulance and return to hospital ... Thank God! The angels got here first ... Thank you Doctor Ruhe and colleague for the expression of sympathy, and*

especially for the prayers that become our shield in the 'age of frustration' as the Guardian described our period.[214]

A few days before, on July 11, 1967, a simple memorial service for Charles was held in Portland. The opening remarks of Conrad Lewis Kerr, who knew Charles well, expressed the inner feelings of all those who knew that noble soul:

We grieve the loss of Charles, our companion on the path, and yet we rejoice that he has been freed from the bonds of mortal existence and has entered the peace of Eternal Kingdom.[215]

Helen's Struggles After Charles' Passing

Adjusting to life without Charles was extremely difficult for Helen—not only emotionally, but also practically. Charles had always taken care of their material needs, including driving, which Helen had never learned.

Financially, Helen was secure, despite the termination of the Bishop Fund, as she had been a careful investor and a regular reader of the Wall Street Journal. However, without Charles' support, she found many of her plans difficult to realize.

She had long dreamed of pioneering, particularly in Hispanic communities, but logistical barriers—her age, health, and the housing market—prevented her from moving forward. In a letter to Roger Dahl, the National Archivist, she wrote:

I no longer feel that Oregon is my home. After Labor Day we began to prepare it for sale before my move to Texas ... the prime [interest] rate precludes a quick sale—so the Realtors and Baháʼís tell me ... [216]

The other obstacle to her plan was the fact that the housing market in Portland did not improve. There were scores of other logistical barriers at that time, such as her age and gender that made moving by herself seem inappropriate.

Much to her regret to the end of her life, Helen's sincere hope for pioneering somewhere for her beloved Faith remained an unrealized dream.

Resignation from the Portland Assembly

On her 70th birthday (1975), Helen resigned from the Portland Baháʼí Spiritual Assembly, writing to the secretary, Mark Freehill. As always, her words are a clear mirror of her heart:

... Praise God I have reached this day ... Assembly meetings come around too soon and last too long. I miss the tone of rising to an occasion—the sweet solemnity—that allowed for some warmth or flashes of wit and wisdom.

Gone is the quest for the intangibles as 'essence' of the human problems. Of course I have been taught that all things here below move forward by stages. Now there is concern with the media and public relations ...

Yet, she reassured the community:

I shall not be content to study the Bahá'í Texts and rummaging in my papers! I am glad to have invitations from the Assembly or Groups wanting a speaker. When the sleeping are awakened they put to me hard questions on the living experience of religion.[217]

The fact was undeniable that during Helen's lifetime, the American Bahá'í community changed in many respects. When she embraced the Faith almost half a century earlier, the U.S. census showed that there were only about 1,247 Bahá'ís in the United States. It was a community whose membership was primarily, but not exclusively, composed of many well-educated and well-to-do individuals, most of whom were of European American descent. Their small number, their common Faith, their devotion to 'Abdu'l-Bahá as the Centre of Covenant, and after Him to Shoghi Effendi as the Guardian of their Faith, were the strong bonds that kept them together truly as a family. Many of them had the extraordinary ability to express their thoughts and feelings through letters that, in those days before the Internet and cell phones, were the main avenue of communication. Many of them stayed connected with one another by correspondence. It is most fortunate that so many of those letters have been preserved in local or the national archives, as well as in family files.

By the time that Helen offered her resignation from the Portland Assembly, the number of Bahá'ís in the United States well exceeded 100,000. The direct and energetic teaching campaigns of the 1960s and 1970s had made the American Bahá'í community significantly more diverse—racially, ethnically, socio-economically, and even culturally. With the growth of her beloved Faith in the US, also came a feeling of great nostalgia for Helen. The intimacy of the bygone era had vanished, but not its memory nor the powerful feelings associated with it:

> *Gone are the candle-lit dinners and quiet hours of fragrant communities experience in the world of the wondrous. Gone is the reverent re-telling of the high and Holy Days bringing into Time a kind of eternity.*[218]

Despite the changing landscape, her love for the Faith never wavered.

Helen Bishop's life was one of unwavering service, resilience, and deep faith. While she mourned the loss of Shoghi Effendi and Charles, she remained committed to the Cause until the end of her days, embracing both the nostalgia of the past and the promise of the future.

Endnotes

[1] Helen Bishop in a letter to Roger Dahl, 14 February 1980, Portland Bahá'í Center Archive.
[2] 'Abdu'l-Bahá, *Tablets of the Divine Plan*, https://www.bahai.org/r/253152980
[3] Ibid., https://www.bahai.org/r/736640944
[4] Ibid., https://www.bahai.org/r/225855160
[5] Letter from May Maxwell to Helen Bishop, 10 June 1926, Portland Bahá'í Center Archive
[6] Louis Gregory in a letter to Helen Bishop, 26 June 1927, Portland Bahá'í Center Archive.
[7] Letter from Louis Gregory to Helen Bishop, 7 June 1926, archive unknown
[8] Letter from May Maxwell to Helen Bishop, 1 June 1926, archive unknown.
[9] Helen Bishop, "The Beloved Returns," *The Bahá'í World: 1940-1944* (vol. IX).
[10] Letter from Helen Bishop to Honor Kempton, 25 June 1935, archive unknown.
[11] Letter from Helen Bishop to Marion Holley, 12 December 1939; the first page of letter found in the Portland Bahá'í Center Archive with this date but not the second page so the quotation could not be verified.
[12] Ibid.
[13] Ibid.
[14] Ibid.
[15] Ibid.
[16] Helen Bishop letter to Honor Kempton, 14 December 1939, archive unknown.
[17] Ibid.
[18] Ibid.
[19] George Latimer notes, Portland Bahá'í Centre Archive.
[20] Hannen, "With 'Abdu'l-Bahá in Dublin, New Hampshire," p. 5.
[21] Letter from May Maxwell to Helen Bishop, 1 June 1926, Portland Bahá'í Center Archive.
[22] Ibid.
[23] Letter from May Maxwell to Helen Bishop, 10 June 1926, Portland Bahá'í Center Archive.
[24] Letter from Louis Gregory to Helen Bishop, 7 June 1926, Portland Bahá'í Centre Archive.
[25] Letter from May Maxwell to Helen Bishop, 27 August 1926, archive unknown.
[26] Ibid.
[27] Mary Maxwell quoted in a letter to her mother, 24 May 1926, quoted in Violette Nakhjavani, *The Maxwells of Montreal, Middle Years 1923-1937*, London UK: George Ronald Pub., 2011.

[28] Letter from May Maxwell to Helen Bishop, Portsmouth, NH, 13 September 1926, Portland Bahá'í Archives.
[29] Letter from May Maxwell to Helen Bishop, 2 July 1926.
[30] Letter from May Maxwell to Helen Bishop, 26 November 1926, archive unknown.
[31] Letter from Mrs Maxwell to Helen Bishop, 23 November 1926.
[32] Ibid.
[33] Ibid.
[34] Letter from May Maxwell to Helen Bishop, 23 June 1927, archive unknown.
[35] Letter from May Maxwell to Helen Bishop, 4 August 1927, archive unknown.
[36] Letter from Louis Gregory to Helen Bishop, from Fellowship House, Eliot, Maine, 9 September 1927, Portland Bahá'í Archives.
[37] Letter from Shoghi Effendi to Helen Bishop, June 1932, archive unknown.
[38] Letter from Shoghi Effendi to Helen Bishop, 23 December 1933, archive unknown.
[39] Letter from Helen Bishop to Marion Holley, 12 December 1939, archive unknown.
[40] Shoghi Effendi, quoted in Hoagg, "Short History of the International Bahá'í Bureau," *Bahá'í World: 1932-1934*, p. 261.
[41] Letter/Cablegram from Shoghi Effendi to the Bishops, 23 October 1933, archive unknown.
[42] Letter from Marion Holly to Helen Bishop, from Visalia, California, 11 February 1934, archive unknown.
[43] Letter from Helen Bishop to Marion Holly, 12 July 1946, archive unknown.
[44] Ibid.
[45] Letter from Helen Bishop to Alfred Lunt, he received it after the National Convention in Chicago in 1934, Barstow Collection, #462, located at https://www.h-net.org/~bahai/docs/vol13/Barstow_451-485.pdf.
[46] Letter on behalf of Shoghi Effendi to Emogene Hoagg, 16 December 1935 and 12 July 1946, archive unknown.
[47] Holley, "Survey," *Bahá'í World: 1934–1936*, p. 41.
[48] Letter on behalf of the Guardian to Helen Bishop, 16 December 1935, archive unknown.
[49] Letter from Helen Bishop to a friend, 29 September 1935, archive unknown.
[50] Helen Bishop, "Geneva Scans the European Community," *Bahá'í World: 1936-38*, p. 110.
[51] Letter from Shoghi Effendi to Helen Bishop, 1 April 1935, archive unknown.
[52] Letter from Shoghi Effendi to Helen Bishop, 24 November 1935, archive unknown.
[53] Helen Bishop, "A Session at the World Congress of Faiths," *The Bahá'í World: 1936-38*, pp. 634-645.
[54] David Hofman, *George Townshend*, p. 150.
[55] Ibid., p. 151.
[56] Ibid., p. 151.
[57] George Townshend quoted in Hofman, *George Townshend*, p. 124-5.
[58] Shoghi Effendi quoted in Hofman, *George Townshend*, p. 126.

[59] Letter from George Townshend to Helen Bishop, 6 April 1936, archive unknown.
[60] Ibid.
[61] Ibid.
[62] Viscount Samuel quoted in Helen Bishop, "A Session of World Congress of Faiths," in *The Bahá'í World: 1936-38*, p. 635.
[63] George Townshend quoted in Bishop, "A session," *The Bahá'í World: 1936-1938*, pp. 636-641.
[64] Ibid., p. 642.
[65] Ibid., p. 643.
[66] Hofman, *George Townshend*, p. 132.
[67] Ibid.
[68] Letter from Shoghi Effendi to Helen Bishop, date and archive unknown.
[69] Personal note of Helen Bishop to her doctor, year unknown, possibly 1951, archive unknown.
[70] Nakhjavani, *The Maxwell's of Montreal*, p. 270.
[71] Hofman, "Annual Report," *The Bahá'í World: 1936-1938*, p. 150.
[72] Letter from Rúhíyyih Khánum to Helen Bishop, 18 April 1937, Portland Bahá'í Center Archive.
[73] Letter from Rúhíyyih Khánum to Helen Bishop, 5 May 1937, Portland Bahá'í Center Archive.
[74] Letter from Marion Holley to Helen Bishop, 10 April 1937, archive unknown.
[75] Letter from Marion Holley to Helen Bishop, 12 May 1937, archive unknown.
[76] Letter from Honor Kempton to Helen Bishop, 30 June 1939, archive unknown.
[77] Ibid.
[78] Letter from Marguerite Sears to Helen Bishop, June 1940, archive unknown.
[79] Letter from Helen Bishop to Shoghi Effendi, 20 August 1946, archive unknown.
[80] Bishop, "In Praise of Words," *The Bahá'í World: 1934-1936*, p. 632.
[81] Ibid, p. 635.
[82] Letter on behalf of Shoghi Effendi to Helen Bishop, dated 18 July 1937, archive unknown.
[83] Letter of HW Boffin to Lady Blomfield, 7 October 1937, archive unknown.
[84] Letter of HW Boffin to Helen Bishop, 9 October 1937, archive unknown.
[85] Letter on behalf of Shoghi Effendi to Helen Bishop, 16 November 1936, archive unknown.
[86] Nakjavani, "The Ten-Year Crusade," *The Journal of Bahá'í Studies*, p. 1.
[87] Letter from Helen Bishop to a friend, 19 October 1941, archive unknown.
[88] Letter from Helen Bishop to Marion Holley, 9 May 1939, Helen Bishop papers, Portland Bahá'í Centre Archive.
[89] Letter from Helen Bishop to Mark Tobey, 27 November 1939, Helen Bishop papers, Portland Bahá'í Center Archive.
[90] Letter from Helen Bishop to Marion Holley, 9 May 1939, Portland Bahá'í Center Archive.
[91] Letter from Mary Maxwell to Helen Bishop, 14 October 1929, archive unknown.
[92] Letter from Horace Holley to Helen Bishop, 1 April 1940, archive unknown.

[93] Letter from Helen Bishop to Dr Salvatore Pablo Lucia, who was also the personal physician of Marion Holley, Halloween 1940, Portland Bahá'í Center Archive.
[94] Letter from Honor Kempton to Helen Bishop, 3 November 1942, archive unknown.
[95] Letter from Shirley Warde to Helen Bishop, 25 June 1939, archive unknown.
[96] Letter from Helen Bishop to Mark Tobey, 27 November 1939, Portland Bahá'í Center Archive.
[97] Letter on behalf of Shoghi Effendi to Honor Kempton, 18 March 1939, Portland Bahá'í Center Archive.
[98] Ibid.
[99] Letter from Honor Kempton to Helen Bishop, 17 March 1939, Portland Bahá'í Center Archive.
[100] Letter from Shoghi Effendi to Honor Kempton, 18 March 1939, Portland Bahá'í Center Archive.
[101] Letter from Honor Kempton to the Bishops, spring of 1941, archive unknown.
[102] Ibid.
[103] Letter from Helen Bishop to Mark Tobey, 14 July 1939, Portland Bahá'í Center Archive. "The Siegfrieds" may imply "the Schopflochers."
[104] Letter from Helen Bishop to Mary Maxwell, 18 July 1939, archive unknown.
[105] Letter from Helen Bishop to Ethel Moore, dated 16 October 1946, archive unknown.
[106] Holley, "International Survey," *The Bahá'í World: 1940-1944*, p. 63.
[107] Letter from Lilian Stevens to Helen Bishop, 14 August 1940 archive unknown
[108] Ibid.
[109] Letter of Helen Bishop to Honor Kempton, 19 May 1941, archive unknown.
[110] Shoghi Effendi, *The Promised Day Is Come*, https://www.bahai.org/r/114413151
[111] Holley, "International Survey," *The Bahá'í World: 1940-1944*, p. 13.
[112] Shoghi Effendi, *The Promised Day Is Come*, https://www.bahai.org/r/495515462
[113] Ibid., https://www.bahai.org/r/940358954
[114] Letter from Helen Bishop to Honor Kempton, 28 February 1941, archive unknown.
[115] Letter from Helen Bishop to the National Teaching Committee, 21 August 1940, archive unknown.
[116] Letter from Helen Bishop to Charlotte Linfoot, 21 August 1940, archive unknown.
[117] Letter from Helen Bishop to Charlotte Linfoot, 9 September 1940, archive unknown.
[118] Letter from Helen Bishop to Robert Gulick, 20 May 1941, Portland Bahá'í Center Archive.
[119] Ibid.
[120] Ibid.
[121] Letter from Alice Anderson to Helen Bishop, May 1941, Portland Bahá'í Center Archive.
[122] Shoghi Effendi, *Messages to America*, p. 39.
[123] Shoghi Effendi, *Messages to Canada*, p. 276.

[124] Letter from Rúhíyyih Khánum to Dr Ali Kuli Khan, 15 April 1940. Ali Kuli and Florence Khan papers, National Bahá'í Archives, United States.
Archivist: Our collection of the Khan papers does not have the original 15 April 1940 letter from Rúhíyyih Khánum. But it does contain a typed page with the extract from the letter. The information about Frances Benedict Stewart pioneering to Argentina is not in the original extract, but was added to identify Mrs Stewart.
Editor: The typed sheet does not say who made the extract and it is not known whether copies of it circulated, so the quote may have come from another source …".

[125] Letter from Marion Holley to Helen Bishop, 2 April 1940, archive unknown. The sentence 'To this day …' originally read 'To this day, I might not have won through the Cause, had she not come to our home.'

[126] Letter from Helen Bishop to Sutherland Maxwell, archive unknown.

[127] Ibid.

[128] Letter from Marion Holley to Helen Bishop, 2 April 1940, archive unknown.

[129] Pilgrim's notes from a letter from Helen Bishop to Mrs Edwina Clifford, 26 February 1943, archive unknown

[130] Shoghi Effendi, *The Advent of Divine Justice*, https://www.bahai.org/r/139916895

[131] Letter from Helen Bishop to Horace Holley, 8 September 1941, Portland Bahá'í Center Archive.

[132] Letter from Helen Bishop to Charlotte Linfoot, 9 April 1942, archive unknown

[133] Holley, "International Survey," *The Bahá'í World: 1940-1944*, pp. 52-53.

[134] Letter from Helen Bishop to her brother Robert, 19 November 1944, archive unknown

[135] Letter from RB Atwood to Horace Holly and the National Spiritual Assembly of the USA, 17 October 1941, quoted in Gilstrap, *From Copper to Gold*, p. 182.

[136] Letter from President J. L. Hartman of Bowling Green Business University to Horace Holly and the National Spiritual Assembly of the USA., 23 October 1941, quoted in Gilstrap, *From Copper to Gold*, p. 183.

[137] These passages may be quoted from two letters to the Guardian in which Helen reported in detail her visit with Sir Alexander; the first was written in April 1944 and the second after the National Convention of 1944 in Chicago and dated 31 May. She may also have written a report to Shoghi Effendi, date unknown, possibly sometime in December 1943, archive unknown.

[138] Ibid.

[139] Ibid.

[140] Ibid.

[141] Ibid.

[142] Ibid.

[143] Ibid.

[144] Ibid., p. 74

[145] Letter from Helen Bishop to Shoghi Effendi, 14 April 1944, archive unknown

[146] Ibid.

[147] Ibid.

[148] Ibid.
[149] Ibid.
[150] Letter from Helen Bishop to Marguerite Welby, 17 April 1944, archive unknown
[151] Shoghi Effendi quoted in Ioas, "Teaching in North America," *The Bahá'í World: 1940-1944*, p. 202; for the complete list of names of the pioneers and the areas of their service in Latin America, see pp. 83-90.
[152] Shoghi Effendi, *This Decisive Hour,* https://www.bahai.org/r/638973491
[153] H Van Buren Magonile quoted in McDaniel, "Temple of Light," *The Bahá'í World: 1940-1944*, p. 173.
[154] Shoghi Effendi, *This Decisive Hour,* https://www.bahai.org/r/806375480
[155] Letter from Helen Bishop to Shoghi Effendi, 14 April 1944, archive unknown.
[156] Letter from Rúhíyyih Khánum on behalf of Shoghi Effendi, archive unknown.
[157] Ibid.
[158] Ibid.
[159] Letter from Helen Bishop to Edna True, 25 October 1944, archive unknown.
[160] Letter from Helen Bishop to Edward R. Stettinius, Secretary of State, 31 December 1944, archive unknown.
[161] Letter from Horace Holley, on behalf of the National Spiritual Assembly, to Helen Bishop, 13 February 1945, archive unknown
[162] Ibid.
[163] Letter from Helen Bishop to Hope and Phil Thurmond, 31 December 1944, Portland Bahá'í Center Archive.
[164] Helen Bishop letter to the Inter-American Committee 2 March 1945, archive unknown.
[165] Helen Bishop, "The Beloved Returns," *The Bahá'í World: 1940-1944*, p. 758.
[166] Ibid.
[167] Ibid., pp. 756-767.
[168] Letter from Helen Bishop to Mark Tobey, 29 November (unclear in the original if is the 29th or something close to it), 1945, Portland Bahá'í Center Archive.
[169] Shoghi Effendi, *Citadel of Faith*, https://www.bahai.org/r/869859223
[170] Ibid., https://www.bahai.org/r/131479941
[171] Helen Bishop delegate report to the Bahá'ís of Pasadena, 1 May 1946, archive unknown.
[172] Letter from Frau Horn to Helen Bishop, 1 July 1945, archive unknown.
[173] Letter from Helen Bishop to Rafi Mottahedeh, 2 April 1946, archive unknown.
[174] Letter from Helen Bishop to Shoghi Effendi, 8 June 1946, archive unknown.
[175] Letter from Helen Bishop to Sarah Walrath, 4 October 1946, Portland Bahá'í Center Archive.
[176] Letter from Shoghi Effendi to Helen Bishop, October 1946, archive unknown.
[177] Pilgrims' notes from Blomfield, *The Chosen Highway*.
[178] 'Abdu'l-Baha quoted in Sims, *Japan Will Turn Ablaze*, p. 51.

[179] Bishop, "His Japanese Witnesses," *The Bahá'í World: 1940-1944*, p. 685.
[180] Ibid., p. 686.
[181] Ibid., p. 688.
[182] Badii, *World Order*, pp. 45-64.
[183] Holley, "International Survey," *The Bahá'í World: 1946-1950*, p.42.
[184] Letter from Helen Bishop to Shoghi Effendi, 13 March 1946, Portland Bahá'í Center Archive.
[185] Letter from Shoghi Effendi to Helen Bishop, 15 December 1948, archive unknown.
[186] Ibid., 30 October 1950. unknown archive
[187] Diary of Helen Bishop, May 1953, archive unknown.
[188] Diary of Helen Bishop, archive unknown.
[189] Helen Bishop, Introduction, Bahá'u'lláh, *The Kitáb-i-Íqán: The Book of Certitude*, translated by Shoghi Effendi (Wilmette, Ill.: Bahá'í Publishing Committee, 1950), p. xv.
[190] Ibid, p. ix.
[191] Ibid, p. xvii.
[192] Ibid, p. xvii.
[193] Letter on behalf of Shoghi Effendi to Helen Bishop, 25 May 1952, archive unknown.
[194] Shoghi Effendi, "The Guardian's Message," *Jubilee Celebration*, p. 5.
[195] Ibid., p. 5.
[196] *National Spiritual Assembly of the Bahá'ís of the United States, Jubilee Celebration*, 29 April - 6 May 1953, p. 12.
[197] Ibid.
[198] Ibid., pp. 12-13.
[199] Ibid., p. 13.
[200] Ibid., p. 13.
[201] Shoghi Effendi, "Portrait of Bahá'u'lláh Sent," *Messages 1950-1957*, p. 146.
[202] Shoghi Effendi, *Citadel of Faith*, https://www.bahai.org/r/073280724
[203] Shoghi Effendi, "A Planetary Spiritual Crusade," *Messages 1950-1957*, pp. 152-3.
[204] Shoghi Effendi, *God Passes By*, https://www.bahai.org/r/106101923
[205] Shoghi Effendi, *The World Order of Bahá'u'lláh*, https://www.bahai.org/r/185571999
[206] Ibid., https://www.bahai.org/r/346244080
[207] Shoghi Effendi, Bahá'í Administration, *World Order*, Volume 12, pp. 341
[208] Diaries of Helen Bishop, archive unknown. Some of this information is in a letter from Helen Bishop to Dr Rexford Parmelee, Secretary of the National Teaching Committee, 20 December 1966.
[209] Cablegram from the Universal House of Justice, on the occasion of Charles Bishop's passing, archive unknown.
[210] Letter from Rouhi Latimer to Helen Bishop, 12 June 1942, archive unknown

[211] Letter from Helen Bishop to Rowland [no surname], 19 October 1941, Portland Bahá'í Center Archive.
[212] Letter from Honor Kempton to Helen Bishop, 17 March 1939, Portland Bahá'í Center Archive.
[213] Letter from Helen Bishop (to whom???) 15 September 1943, archive unknown.
[214] Letter from Helen Bishop to Charlotte Linfoot, 20 July 1967, archive unknown
[215] Eulogy for Charles Bishop by Conrad Lewis Kerr, archive unknown.
[216] Letter from Helen Bishop to Arthur Dahl, 14 February 1980, Portland Bahá'í Center Archive.
[217] Letter from Helen Bishop to Mark Freehill, 19 July 1975, Portland Bahá'í Center Archive.
[218] Letter from Helen Bishop to Roger Dahl, 14 February 1980, Portland Bahá'í Center Archive.